Great Paint Finishes for a GORGEOUS HOME

Great Paint Finishes for a GORGEOUS HOME

GARY LORD

NORTH LIGHT BOOKS
CINCINNATI, OHIO

A NOTE ABOUT SAFETY

Due to the toxicity concerns, most art and craft material manufacturers have begun labeling their products with proper health warnings or nontoxic seals. It is always important to read a manufacturer's label when using a product for the first time. Follow any warnings about not using the product when pregnant or contemplating pregnancy, about keeping the product out of the reach of children or about incompatible products. Always work in a well-ventilated room when using products with fumes.

The information in this book is presented in good faith, but no warranty is given, nor results guaranteed, nor is freedom from any patent to be inferred. Since we have no control over physical conditions surrounding the application of products, techniques and information herein, the publisher and author disclaim any liability for results.

Great Paint Finishes for a Gorgeous Home. Copyright © 1998 by Gary Lord. Manufactured in China. All rights reserved. No part of this book may be reproduced in any form or by any electronic or mechanical means including information storage and retrieval systems without permission in writing from the publisher, except by a reviewer, who may quote brief passages in a review. Published by North Light Books, an imprint of F&W Publications, Inc., 1507 Dana Avenue, Cincinnati, Ohio 45207. (800) 289-0963. First paperback edition 2002.

Other fine North Light Books are available from your local bookstore, art supply store or direct from the publisher.

06 05 04 03 02   5 4 3 2 1

Library of Congress has catalogued hardcover edition as follows:

Lord, Gary
Great paint finishes for a gorgeous home / by Gary Lord.
    p.   cm.
Includes bibliographical references and index.
ISBN 0-89134-822-0 (hardcover)
    1. House painting. 2. Interior decoration. 3. Finishes and finishing. I. Title.
TX323.L67   1998
698'.14—dc21   98-18154
ISBN 1-58180-294-3 (pbk. : alk. paper)   CIP

Edited by Karen Spector
Production edited by Marilyn Daiker
Designed by Brian Roeth
Photography on pages 42 and 96 by Ron Forth Photography, Boulder, Colorado
Photography on page 74 by Joe Van de Hatert and LaNier Pratt of Audible Elegance

ABOUT THE AUTHOR

Gary Lord received a B.F.A. from Ohio State University in 1974. In 1975 he opened Gary Lord Wall Options and Associates in Cincinnati, and he is still creating the whole spectrum of decorative paint finishes on a national level.

Besides owning and operating his business, Gary is also contributing editor for the Home Decor Article in *Decorative Artist Workbook, Painting,* and *Artistic Stenciler.* His work has appeared in many national magazines including: *Traditional Building, Home, Better Homes and Gardens, Interiors,* and *1001 Decorating Ideas.* Gary also writes articles for many regional and local magazines such as *Architectural Living* and *Builder/Architect.*

He has appeared on the national Home and Garden Network television show *Decorating with Style.* He has filmed fifteen segments which have aired collectively over one hundred times. He also appears on many regional television shows such as *Around the House* and *The Hardware Store Show.*

In 1995 Gary and his colleague, David Schmidt, opened Prismatic Painting Studio. Students from around the world have attended their school. To get more information about the school and other things Gary is up to, see the listing for the school on page 124 or contact him by e-mail at info@prismaticpainting.com or visit their Web site at www.prismaticpainting.com.

Gary lives in Cincinnati with his wife Marianne and his children Ben, Corrie, and Jared.

DEDICATION

I wish to thank, first, my mother whom I watched for endless hours as a child do one art project after another. It was because of her that I developed a love for the arts. I grew up at the kitchen table learning color theory, how to mix paints and use brushes, how to draw and more. But most importantly, I learned the value of giving a handmade project to others and the joy in making it as well as giving it away.

ACKNOWLEDGMENTS

In my professional career I wish to thank the many clients, interior designers, architects and my students who enable me to make a living in one of the most rewarding ways I can think of.

I wish to make a special thanks to the following people: my wife Marianne, for her endless, unwavering support of me in all my endeavors and for being my partner in life as well as in business and also for her endless hours of typing and retyping for this book. To my children Ben, Corrie and Jared who are my biggest successes in life. To my fellow artisans who continue to help me learn and grow in this field and whose work is instrumental in this book: Mike Schmidt, Dave Schmidt, George Neumann, Jeff Paul, Helen Ryan, Kathleen Lichtendahl, Liz Fortino, Joe Taylor and George Kitta. Thank you to Gary McCauley, Ron Forth and others for their wonderful photographs. Thank you also to my publisher and especially to Adam Blake for his assistance in getting the book done. I also want to thank the people from Faux Effects, Benjamin Moore and Ritins of Canada for the use of their products.

Thank you to Michael Couch, June Surber and Frank Puntenney whose wonderful sense of interior design and creativity made many of the projects in this book happen. A special thanks to my clients who allowed their beautiful homes to be photographed. Thank you to Audible Elegance for their photographs of the Dziersk's home.

CREDITS

Special thanks to my clients who were kind enough to let me photograph their homes for this book:

Mr. and Mrs. Kennedy

Mr. and Mrs. Sirkin

Mr. and Mrs. Koesters

Mr. and Mrs. Dziersk

Mr. and Mrs. Gorelick

Table of Contents

Introduction
— 1 0 —

Part 1
BEFORE YOU GET
STARTED
— 1 2 —

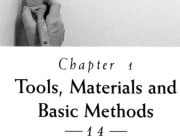

Chapter 1
Tools, Materials and
Basic Methods
— 1 4 —

Part 2
PROJECTS
— 2 4 —

Chapter 2
Two-Color Rag Blend
— 2 6 —

Chapter 3
Waterfall
— 3 0 —

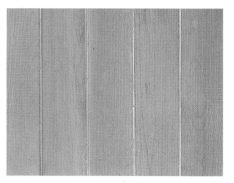

Chapter 4
Lightening Up
Dark Paneling
— 3 6 —

Chapter 5
Newsprint
— 4 2 —

Chapter 6
Crackle Finish
— 4 8 —

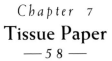

Chapter 7

Tissue Paper

— 5 8 —

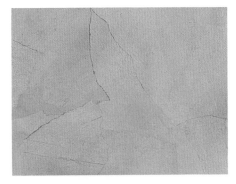

Chapter 8

Torn Paper

— 6 6 —

Chapter 9

Stone Block

— 7 4 —

Chapter 10

Sand Drift

— 8 2 —

Chapter 11

Metallic Textured Finish

— 9 0 —

Chapter 12

Wall Striping

— 9 6 —

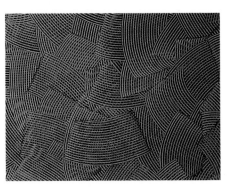

Chapter 13

Combing

— 1 0 4 —

Part 3

A GALLERY OF GORGEOUS FINISHES

— 1 1 2 —

Resources

— 1 2 4 —

Glossary

— 1 2 6 —

Index

— 1 2 7 —

Introduction

I can think of no more enjoyable way to decorate a home or office than with a hand-painted finish of some sort. Since the beginning of time, society has valued a hand-painted finish as an alternative to other forms of decorating. We have proof from the caves in Alsace-Lorraine in France that prehistoric man brought his world into his home with cave paintings. We have had different art styles throughout history: the petroglyphs, Egyptian, Greco-Roman and Renaissance, up to modern styles. We are all using many of the same techniques and effects today that prior generations of artists perfected. For centuries, though, decorative painting techniques were kept as "trade secrets," with artisans working behind closed doors or shielded by screens so no one could learn their techniques. The information was often passed on only to family members and sometimes information was lost forever. But today many of those "Old World" decorative painting techniques are being shared by authors and schools throughout the world.

In this book you will learn many valuable painting skills with easy, step-by-step instructions accompanied by detailed photographs showing you the way. Don't be afraid to try anything in this book. The worst thing that can happen is you lose a little of your time and have to repaint an area. Even if you make a mistake, think of it not as a failure but as an opportunity to learn. I can't tell you how many of my own jobs don't go the way I think they will, and I have to change course in midstream. Often, some of my best work comes out of the jobs that were failures

in the beginning. Go out and learn as much as you can by reading more books, taking classes and practicing. My hope is that by the time you finish reading this book, you will want to try a project in every room of your house.

Part 1

BEFORE YOU GET STARTED

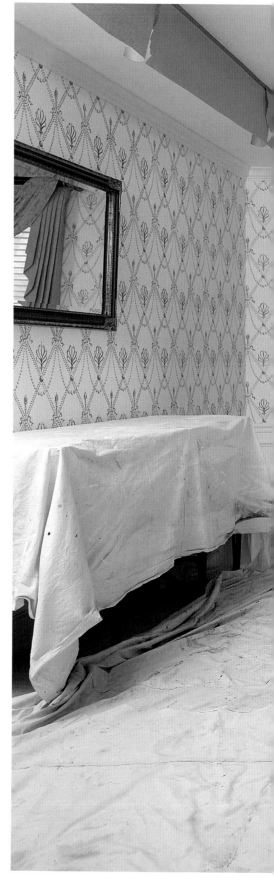

It will save you headaches in the long run if you take time at the beginning of your project to gather all the materials you'll need and properly prepare your room for painting.

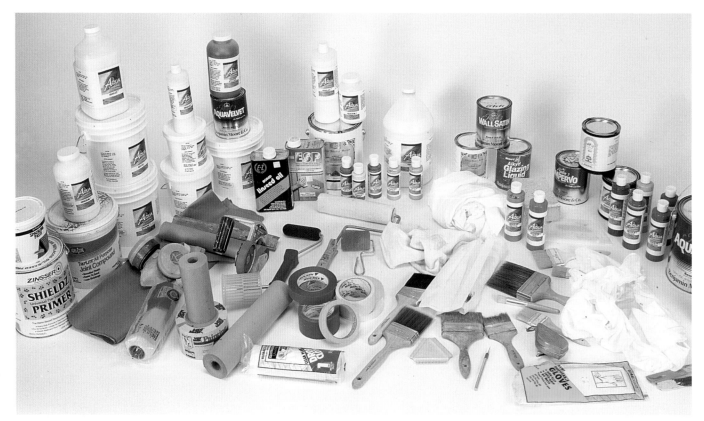

You probably already have many of the tools and materials you need to create the finishes in this book.
Take stock of what you have and use this chapter to decide what else you need to buy.

Chapter 1
Tools, Materials and Basic Methods

As in any career in life, the better the tools you have to execute your job, the better off you are. In the long run, the right tool for the right job will not only save you time and money, but will also give you a more professional-looking job. It will also make your work go more easily and allow you to have more fun. Most of the tools and materials listed below are not expensive, and you may already own a number of them. Some of the more expensive items will be your brushes.

You need a variety of brush sizes to properly re-create the decorative paint finishes shown in this book.

BRUSHES

In order to execute the best finish possible, you need to buy the best brushes you can afford for that particular finish. The better your brushes, the better your results will be. An inexpensive brush will not last long and will almost always give you an inferior look. If you take good care of your brushes, and all the tools mentioned in this book, they will last for many years.

Brush Size

You will find that your job will go a lot faster if you have a variety of brush sizes. Use the correct size brush for the area

you are working. If you are working around a door frame that is very close to the adjacent wall, don't try to smash a 4-inch brush into that area. Instead, use a small artist's brush or a small 1-inch brush that will fit the area. Vice versa, don't use a small 1-inch brush to cut in your base or glaze coat around the large open areas in a room. Use a 2- to 4-inch brush. The size and quality of your brush will often be a factor in how good your finish looks.

Pro Tips
- Even high-quality brushes may shed hairs so it is good practice to break in all new brushes by using them for priming and general prep work rather than finish work until all the loose hairs have come out.
- In general, do not use a latex brush in an oil-based paint because the strong solvents may damage your brush. Likewise, do not use oil brushes in a water-based paint because the water will explode the natural hairs in the brush and ruin its fine quality.

Brush Quality

As in centuries ago, good quality brushes are often hand-crafted from a variety of materials. Brushes used for water-based paints are usually made from synthetics such as a nylon or polyester blend. Oil-based paint brushes are often made of pig or ox hair. You want to make sure that your brush has a nice chiseled edge and will hold a fair amount of paint to work with. The price of brushes will often indicate how good they are. Frequently, the axiom "you get what you pay for" applies. However, it is not always true. In the beginning, buy the best brushes you can afford and then experiment with different, less expensive brushes.

Chip Brushes

In the decorative painting field, I feel that perhaps the best all-purpose brush is the chip brush. It comes in a variety of sizes and is usually made of white China bristle (pig) hair. These brushes are very inexpensive ($.79 up to $2 depending on the size), and you can use them in both latex and oil paints. I use them a tremendous amount in my own work, and when one becomes worn or damaged I can get a new one for another $.79. These brushes do tend to shed hairs when new, so be careful how and where you use them until the hairs stop shedding. When I first use a new chip brush, I flick the hairs back and forth for a minute to remove any loose hairs. I will then use the chip brush as a pouncing brush to even out the glaze along moldings and corners of a room for two to three rooms. By then, the brush

If you don't already have some, you need to buy chip brushes in various sizes. They are inexpensive and versatile.

has lost whatever hairs it may lose, and I can use it to brush on my glazes or cut in a room as well as still use it for a pouncing brush.

PAINTS

Most paint colors in oil and latex are made from ground-up pigments derived from a natural source, though some pigments are made from synthetic materials. These ground-up, dried pigments are put into a binding solution that carries and fixes the pigment. As the binding solution evaporates, the pigments dry to a protective film. The film has solvents or thinners that can dilute the mixture for workability. The paint is then soluble in a variety of mediums such as water, paint thinner, xylene, and lacquer thinner.

Until very recently master craftsmen and their apprentices prepared most of their paints. These craftsmen would mix and grind pigments for each individual job. They would keep precise formulas on how they made each individual color so that they could remake it if need be. Even so, it was difficult to remake a batch of paint identical to the one before, so they were always careful to make up enough for each job. Computer-aided color matching is now available, so if you need to touch up a paint finish several years after its initial application, you can get an exact match from your local paint supplier.

Since this book was first published, Benjamin Moore paints has changed their numbering system by which they identify paints. You will need to cross match the numbers used in this book with your Benjamin Moore dealer to get the newest numbers and paints.

COLOR

Today, thanks to highly technical paint manufacturers such as Benjamin Moore, we can choose from a wide variety of paint colors that can be consistently reproduced. Also, with the use of the color-matching computer systems, we can get colors computer-matched and made for us just as easily as buying a standard paint color. This is a tremendous benefit if you need to make an exact color match from fabric, wallpaper or custom paint mix for your project.

If you are new to color theory, you can read books or take a class on the subject; however, it is probably a good idea to get a color wheel and practice making up different colors yourself.

Choosing a Color

Choose a color that relates well to the room conditions. You should take into consideration both natural and artificial lighting in the room as well as the room's furniture, carpet, pictures and fabrics. Always remember that darker colors in a room bring the walls in and are more intimate, while lighter colors recede and the room appears more open.

Once you know something about the room you are painting, you are more likely to make a successful choice from a color card or a bundle of swatches. There is no better way to ensure you have chosen the correct color than painting a sample board that you can move around to see how the color looks under the room's varying light conditions.

The texture and sheen of the finish also affect the color. For example, you can create a beautiful decorative paint finish by using exactly the same shade of color but allowing one paint to be in a flat sheen and another to be in a gloss. You can paint walls in a stripe pattern this way. You can also rag, sponge or feather dust them to create a beautiful, subtle finish much like a damask material.

Combining Color

When it comes to combining color in a decorative scheme, many people are hesitant. In combining colors, as in many other aspects of decoration, observation is important. Inspiration comes from successful color schemes you see in books and magazines but also from fabric patterns and paintings in the room in which you are working. Examples of good color combinations are everywhere. You should train yourself to look for interesting color combinations and then ask yourself what makes them work.

In the twentieth century, there has been an endless variety of colors used in decorating. A desire for muted intense colors and metallics seems to be popular again. Although every decade has had its own particular vogue colors, white and off-whites are persistent color themes.

Color Mixing

Despite the wide range of shades of ready-mixed paints available today, you can achieve a greater degree of subtlety and variety by mixing your own colors. Color mixing is something of an art and requires a lot of practice and a good eye. If you are just learning about color theory, it is best to get a color wheel and practice making up different colors, varying these hues and values until you begin to understand what pigments it takes to create certain colors.

Color Theory

Color theory is a very complex and intricate part of decorative painting. There are many books devoted especially to color theory, and they go into much more detail than I can in this book. For those that are new to color theory, I would recommend taking a class on color theory and reading books on that topic.

WATER-BASED PAINT SYSTEM

Water-based paints are a lot more user-friendly than oil-based paints because they are almost odorless and dry quickly (usually within two hours), allowing for multiple applications in one day. They also clean up very easily with soap and water. They are also a lot healthier for you to use because they do not release harmful toxins into the air while you are using them. There are many parts of the country that are now restricting the use of solvent-based paints because they are not as environmentally friendly as water-based products. It is for all these reasons that most of the paints mentioned in this book are water-based.

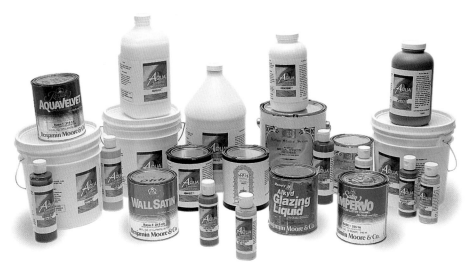

Glazes are cut with products like these to achieve just the right translucency and color.

Base Coat

Most of the time you will use a low-luster or semigloss latex or acrylic paint as your base coat. This will seal the wall surface so that you can manipulate your glaze paint and keep a wet edge as you are working. It also allows you to have a more durable product that gives you a surface that is easier to keep clean.

Glazes

Most water-based glazes are available in two different ways. One way is to mix standard latex paint with an extender such as Aquaglaze or Ritins Special Effects Extender. When added to a standard latex paint color, it will increase the drying time of the product. The longer your glaze paint stays wet on the surface, the easier it is to work your entire wall surface.

Each manufacturer will have its own recommended formula for adding extender to the paint. These formulas may even vary depending on the climate you live in. For example, you may need more

extender in a hot, dry climate than in an area that has a cool, humid climate. If your glaze is drying too fast, add more extender.

Because this method uses standard latex-based paints, the glaze has a little more opacity to it than if you use a clear glazing medium and add tint or colorant to it. The benefit to this method is that your paint store can mix the color of your choice, and you can go back and get exactly the same color time and time again.

The second way to create a water-based glaze is to use a clear glazing vehicle (like Aquacreme or Ritins Scumble Glaze) and add tint or colorant to it. With these products you are able to achieve a more transparent film of color where you may want just a fine sheen film of color over another. It is best to tint Aquacreme or Ritins with artist acrylics but you can also use universal tints. It is rare that you would ever need to thin these glazes because of the way they are manufactured, but if you want to thin them, use water to do so.

Pro Tips

* You cannot apply normal latex-based paints over oil-based paints because they will not bind to each other.
* There are water-based paint products made specifically to bond over oil-based products. One such product is Aquabond.
* You can use an oil-based product over a latex product with no compatibility problems.
* To find out if your walls are now oil or latex, take a cotton swab with rubbing alcohol on it and rub it on an obscure area of the wall. If the paint comes off or gets sticky, it is latex. If it stays hard to firm, it is an oil-based product.

OIL-BASED PAINT SYSTEM

Oil-based paints are traditionally what decorative painters have used for centuries to do their finishes. For that reason, I do describe how to do a few finishes in an oil-based system. In the past, the benefit of an oil-based paint was its slower drying time. This allowed the artist to work an area longer without incurring lap marks or indications of starting and stopping areas in a finish. Also, the translucency of oil-based paints and their solvents were superior to water-based products. This is no longer true with the advances in the water-based paint market. Try the glazes in this book and see how easily and wonderfully they work for you.

Base Coat

It is rare, even if I am using an oil-based glaze, that I base coat walls in an oil-based paint. I can still use my low-luster latex and seal the walls to glaze on, thus avoiding all the toxins and clean-up hassles associated with using oil-based paints. Therefore, I do use latex low-luster paint whenever possible. Even if the existing base coat on the wall is oil, I can still use a water-based product by buying one that will bond to the oil-based product. There are now many paint manufacturers that make a variety of latexes that bond to oil. You should have no trouble finding one.

Glazes

For years I used oil-based glazes for decorative paint finishes. I still use them on occasion for a particular finish or in large areas. To make a generalized oil glaze use: one part ready-mixed oil glazing medium; one part oil-based paint of the color and sheen of your choice; and one part paint thinner.

If your glaze is drying too fast, add a

Pro Tips

* Always test any glaze, either latex or oil, to be sure its consistency and translucency are what you require.
* If the glaze does not hold its design on the wall, you can thicken it up by using more of the glazing medium or the paint itself.
* If you can't see the wall color well through the glaze, add more glazing medium or its solvent to thin it out.
* The depth of color of your glaze is affected directly by how much colorant you put into the glaze. For a more translucent glaze, use less colorant.
* When making up a glaze, do not use all of your paint at once in case you need to adjust the glaze's thickness or transparency.
* Once your glaze is right in all respects, make sure you have enough to finish the whole room.
* All glazes, both oil and water, will thicken up if the container is left open for about twelve hours. (The actual amount of time required will vary depending on the environment.) Seal your container of glaze to prevent this from happening.

There are additional considerations when using oil-based products. Be extremely careful with rags that have oil-based paints or linseed oil on them. It is best to neutralize any linseed oil-soaked rags in water before you let them dry out.

little boiled linseed oil. You can buy linseed oil in the paint store; it comes either boiled or raw. Please note that linseed oil can yellow a light-color finish. It dries more slowly than the paint film and seeps up through the paint film resulting in a yellowing of light colors.

Be careful with all rags that have any

oil glazing on them because they have a possibility of spontaneous combustion. This is especially true if you use linseed oil in your glaze. Allow rags to dry out in an open area without bunching them together. You can also throw them in a bucket of water, which neutralizes them.

SHEEN

Besides choosing between water- or oil-based paints, you must also choose the degree of sheen you want when your paint dries. The paint that has no sheen is called a flat or matte finish. The ones that have a slight sheen are satin, low-luster or eggshell. Other sheens are known as semigloss and high-gloss. All major paint stores will have a sheen chart you can look at to help you determine the sheen you want.

It is generally true that the higher the sheen of paint, the higher the durability and washability of the surface. The negative side of using higher gloss paint on your walls is that it will magnify all your surface defects such as nail pops, bad tape joints, lumps, dents and undulations. Flat paints on walls do not generally clean up well but will hide flaws. So, for good washable durability, I recommend using low-luster sheen on walls. This will not magnify defects and cleans up very well. For additional protection, you can also clear-coat your surface with a clear sealer. This is not normally necessary but some prefer it.

Pro Tips

* A negative application is defined as taking paint away from a surface that has not yet dried. A positive application is defined as adding paint to a surface.
* The sheen normally recommended for your base coat in a negative application is a low-luster or semigloss because it is less absorbent than a flat sheen and is also a more durable finish.
* You can use a flat sheen or any other sheen when doing positive application finishes such as sponging, feather dusting and ragging.

Amount of Paint Needed

Most major paint manufacturers will indicate on their cans how much square footage a gallon covers (usually 300-400 square feet).

For a standard one-color glazing application in a $12' \times 12' \times 8'$ room that has 384 square feet of wall space, about three-quarters of a gallon of made-up glaze will do with a little left over.

I buy one quart of latex paint in the color that I want to use and add two to six parts water-based extender depending on conditions.

If I am using oil, I buy one quart of oil paint, and add one part alkyd glazing medium and one part paint thinner. This gives me more than enough for this sized room.

If you think you may run out of paint before you finish your job, make sure you have enough to do the wall you are starting on. Make your paint change in a corner so it won't be as noticeable if there is any difference.

Sealers

In the past when I used mostly oil-based glazing mediums for my decorative painting techniques, I found little need to seal my finished product for extra protection. The oil-based glazed surface, once it is fully cured (approximately thirty days after painting), can be cleaned very easily with any ammoniated cleaner such as Formula 409 or Fantastic. Just spray your cleaning cloth and wipe down the area you wish to clean. If I were to seal an oil-based glazing system, one of the reasons might be to add extra protection to very high-flow traffic areas like kitchens and foyers or to even out sheen irregularities. You may also want to use a sealer to add more depth of finish to the project.

To seal my oil-based walls, I can use either an oil varnish or oil polyurethane. I can also use a water-based sealer if the

---

Pro Tips

* The best way to apply any of your sealers is to spray them for a nice even application, though this is seldom practical for most people.
* The second best way is to roll the sealer on with a low-nap roller cover. Sometimes bubbles will form on your surface as you roll the sealer on, so you may need to brush the bubbles out while the surface is still wet.

---

manufacturer states it will bond to oil-based paints. You need to be aware that these products will help protect your surface and add greater depth to your finish, but the oil products will also amber or yellow the surface over time. This is especially noticeable on light-colored finishes. Ask your paint dealer which oil sealers will amber less than others. If you want something that ambers very little, if at all, you can try a water-based polyurethane. Not only can you apply these to your water-based glazes, but you can also apply them over many oil-glazed surfaces. Again, ask your paint store for recommendations.

I am finding with my water-based glaze finishes that once they are cured (thirty days), they are mildly washable but not scrubbable. If you want extra protection on a water-based finish, you can use either the oil- or water-based sealers. The sealers come in a variety of sheens—flat, low-luster, semigloss and high-gloss—which affect the ultimate look of your project. I usually seal my walls in a low-luster and if I am doing any moldings or columns, I use a semi- or high-gloss sealer. A note of caution in using water-based sealers: Although they do not amber with age, they create a bluish haze over darker colors. This happens immediately.

CLEANING YOUR TOOLS

It is best to clean up your tools before any paint dries and hardens on them. Once that happens, you will have a much harder time cleaning them, if you can even save them at all. For oil-based paints, I wear rubber gloves not only while doing my decorative finish but also when cleaning up at the end of the day. I have three pots of paint thinner: clean, medium-dirty and dirty. I rinse all my tools first in the dirty thinner. I then rinse them in the medium-dirty thinner, and I do my final cleanup in the clean thinner. Over time you will find the clean thinner becomes medium-dirty and the medium-dirty becomes dirty thinner. I store each of these in its own container and let each one sit for weeks or months, so that the oil sludge settles to the bottom of the container and the paint thinner floats on the top. This occurs even in your dirtiest thinner. When the sludge has settled to the bottom, I slowly pour out the thinner on top through a strainer into a clean container. This is how I continually replenish my clean thinner supply.

With water-based paints, I rinse my tools under running water, soap them up and work the paint out. I then rinse them thoroughly. Hang your brushes with the bristles pointing down to store them.

Storage and Labeling

All paints should be kept in a cool, dry area and never allowed to freeze. Do not store your paints in your garage unless it is heated. The rims of your paint cans should be kept clean so the lids will seal properly when reapplied. Use a felt-tip marker to label all cans of paint with the date, name of paint, paint formula if it is a computer-matched color, what it was used for (base coat on walls, trim color, etc.) and in what room it was used. In five years, if you need to touch up your walls for any reason, you will be very happy that you did this.

Keep three pots of paint thinner if you plan to tackle many projects. Keep one pot of clean paint thinner, one pot of medium-dirty paint thinner and one pot of dirty paint thinner. Renew your clean paint thinner supply by straining the paint sludge out of the dirty paint thinner.

Cleanup is simple with water-based paints.

Pro Tips
* After your brushes are clean, put them back into their brush covers to help them maintain their natural shape.
* Once your small artist brushes are clean, you can return them to their natural shape by using a little soap on your fingers and reshaping them. When you are ready to use the brushes again, simply wash them out with water.

SURFACE AND ROOM PREPARATION

Correct surface and room preparation are crucial to getting a professional look upon completion. Even though it takes time on the front end to prepare a room properly for paint, it saves twice as much time on the back end in cleaning up and fixing any noticeable defects that you can see through your paint finish.

Surface Preparation

General surface preparation should start with a close inspection of the areas you are painting. You want to look for: any nail pops, stress cracks, dings or dents in the walls, previous patching jobs, loose or bad caulking around moldings, flaking or cracking paint, water marks, smoke damage or dirty surfaces, among other things. Make sure you do these inspections while the lighting in the room is good, as it is very easy to miss spots in poor lighting. You could also use a halogen lamp and shine it on your surfaces to help find any problem areas. Usually when I am making my inspection, I use small pieces of blue low-tack adhesive tape to mark any areas in need of repair. I also keep this tape by the areas being repaired until the repair work is complete, because it is often hard to see your spackled spots on white walls. Please note that you should not begin repairing the walls until you have completed the room preparation mentioned in the next section.

Room Preparation

The next step you need to take after your inspection is to protect your floors, trim, ceiling and furniture in the room.

Protecting the Floors

Cover the floors with drop cloths. Use butyl rubber-backed drop cloths so paint can't soak through them.

For hardwood floors or wall-to-wall carpet, I tape out (cover) the baseboards using a tape dispenser and 6- to 12-inch kraft paper that extends beyond the baseboard to cover the edge of the floor. This saves me a tremendous amount of cleanup in the long run. Even though I put drop cloths over the entire floor, they tend to pull away from the wall allowing the floor to be exposed to the risk of paint spatters. The paper shield helps protect the floors from paint spatters even if the drop cloth shifts positions.

Protecting Trim and Ceilings

If I am doing my base coat, I will not mask out the trim and ceiling areas. I just cut into them with my cut brush. But if I am applying a decorative paint finish—which can be messier—I protect these areas using 2-inch blue tape on the trim and for the ceilings either 3-inch easy-mask or 6-inch kraft paper applied using my tape gun and 1-inch blue tape.

Protecting Furniture

I try to move all small pieces of furniture and pictures out of the room. I throw 9′ × 12′ sheets of plastic over all of the furniture remaining in the room. This may sound like a lot of work, but I have found that if you paint often enough, you will spill paint at some point. It is better to be safe than sorry. In my career I have spilled paint dozens of times but because of my good prep work, I have never had to buy a carpet or piece of furniture.

Surface Repair

Once you prep the room, you can then attend to the areas that need repair. If the walls are dirty or greasy, I wash them first. You can use a product like Soilax or TSP to clean the surfaces. Make sure you clean the walls from the floor up to the ceiling. When you clean this way you avoid streaking the walls with cleaning solution. I have had to wash walls very seldom; most of the time a good wall primer will eliminate the need for washing walls. If you have bare drywall, you need to lightly dust the walls before you prime them to make sure your paint will bond properly to the drywall board.

Repairing Cracking Paint

Next, I scrape any loose or cracking paint and then use spackling compound and a putty knife to fill any surface irregularities. Most compounds shrink a little, so leave more on the surface to account for this possible shrinkage. Once the areas are dry, sand them with medium and then fine sandpaper. Sometimes it is easier to feel the texture with your hands than to see it with your eyes. You can spot-prime these areas if there are only a few, but if there are a lot it is sometimes easier just to prime the whole wall.

Repairing Caulking

If the caulking is bad, I remove any loose areas and recaulk with a good tube of paintable acrylic caulking. It is worth buying the better caulking product because it lasts longer than the inexpensive brands.

Pro Tips

* Primers can be tinted to your base coat color and may save you extra coats of paint later on.
* If your walls are in very bad shape, it may be best to call in a professional painter. They have the right skills and proper tools to do the job quickly and professionally.

Base Coating Techniques

When base coating your walls in a water-based paint, use a 2½-inch sash brush to cut in around the edges of the room and around the moldings. If working by yourself, you can cut and roll the walls at the same time. If you are working with another person, one can cut in while the other rolls the paint on.

Use a 9-inch roller frame with a ½-inch-nap lambskin roller cover to apply the paint. The lambskin covers are more expensive but they hold a lot of paint, spatter very little and clean up very quickly. Try to roll right into the wet cut lines as closely as you can on all the edges. You can even turn the roller sideways at the ceiling and baseboards. This avoids the difference you may notice with brushstrokes versus roller marks. Also there is sometimes a minor color difference between paint that has been brushed on versus rolled on, and it will help eliminate that. I almost always apply two solid base coats before doing a decorative finish. You need to make sure the paint has dried thoroughly between coats and before you start your decorative finish.

If I am using oil-based paint for my base coat (which is almost never), I cut and roll the room in the same way. The only thing I do differently is change the roller cover to a ⅜-inch-nap spatterless cover. It is well worth the extra money you spend on a good dripless/spatterless paint cover because of the time it saves you during cleanup. I rinse out my brush and tools in paint thinner, but I will throw the paint cover away if used with oil-based paint.

Glaze Coating Techniques

There are many ways to apply your glazes in decorative paint finishes, from using brushes and paint rollers of all sizes, rags and cheesecloth, to spraying and other techniques. If using a paint roller, I normally use a ⅜-inch dripless cover on a 9-inch roller frame. Each step in the glazing process, from its application to its completion, affects the final look. In this book, I will describe many different ways to apply your glazes.

One of the most important things in your decorative painting process is consistency. Make sure the process is the same throughout. If you are using two or more people to do a finish, make sure each person does the same job throughout to help maintain this consistency. For example, the same person who rolls on the glaze should do it everywhere while the other person takes the glaze off with a rag. Pay close attention to all your edges and corners (which should be masked off before glazing the room), and use a 2-inch chip brush to pounce your glaze in these areas and even it out.

Use a 2½-inch sash brush to cut in the edges of your walls.

Use your roller to apply most of the paint to your walls. Make sure to roll into the cuts while they are still wet.

Practically anything that can hold paint can be used in a decorative paint finish. Here are some common items used.

Part 2
PROJECTS

The door is open, and you are invited in to try one or all of the projects in the next twelve chapters. You should feel free to use the techniques shown while varying the colors to suit the needs of your home. Please note that color values in the photographs of paint finishes show slightly different than they would actually appear if you were standing in the room. If you are attempting to copy a finish exactly as it appears in this book, you may need to experiment a little with the colors. It is always best to test any paint finish on a board before you commit it to your walls. That way you can carry the board throughout your room to see how the paint looks under various light conditions. Also, please remember to use caution when trying out new products. Always be careful to read the warning labels, and be sure to work in a well-ventilated room. For the project in chapter six, you may even want to wear a respirator.

You can modify the technique used in this foyer, or any other technique in the book, to best suit your decorating needs.

To create this look, you actually affix crumpled tissue paper to your walls.

You can add a stencil over any paint finish to enhance the visual appeal. This fleur-de-lis stencil was painted over a tissue paper finish.

Even with sparse decorating, this finish warms a room and delivers added visual interest.

Two-Color Rag Blend

This is perhaps my largest selling technique at the time of writing this book. It is a soft blending technique that goes with almost any style of decorating whether it is contemporary, transitional or traditional. It is also quick to execute so the cost per room is at the low end of decorative paint finishes. You can do this treatment in many color combinations, and it is always very attractive.

You can also blend two to four colors on the wall at the same time, wet into wet, and be able to pull in more than one accent color in just one pass around the room. This is a far quicker treatment to execute than making individual passes around the room for each accent color.

PREPARATION

Base your walls in a color you desire. For this project I used Benjamin Moore #1215 Aquavelvet latex paint. Let the paint dry. Once it is dry, mix up your glazes. If you plan to use the colors from this project, use Aquaglaze with the Benjamin Moore #1197 Aquavelvet and Benjamin Moore #1028 Aquavelvet in your two 1-gallon buckets. Roll the glazes onto your walls about fifty-fifty of each color. Blend them a little wet into wet on the wall while applying them. Work an area about three to four feet square with your glaze leaving a wet edge as you paint. Now use your cotton rag and in a hit-skip pattern of movement with your hand, remove part of your glaze. This will blend the two colors together more on the wall and leave you with a very soft technique.

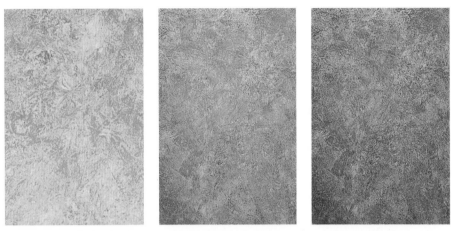

Blend two colors of your choice over a dried base coat to achieve this rag finish.

MATERIALS
- Benjamin Moore #1215 Aquavelvet
- Benjamin Moore #1197 Aquavelvet
- Benjamin Moore #1028 Aquavelvet
- Aquaglaze
- 4-inch chip brush
- 2 empty 1-gallon buckets
- 2 3-inch rollers
- 1 9-inch roller handle
- Paint tray
- 2-inch blue tape
- Cotton rags
- Gloves

Pro Tips
- ✿ Blend two colors together on the wall while wet.
- ✿ Avoid strong compositions. You want a soft blended pattern.
- ✿ Use a chip brush in your corners to even out the glaze.

STEP 1. Base coat your walls in a base paint like Benjamin Moore Aquavelvet. The color shown here is Benjamin Moore #1215 in a low-sheen latex. Allow to dry.

STEP 2. Use either a 3-inch roller or a 4-inch chip brush to apply each color. Use one brush or roller for each color you are applying. Be sure to apply the colors in a small 3- to 5-inch pattern. Cover about 60 percent of the wall space with your first glaze color. In this case, I am using a mixture of one-third Benjamin Moore #1197 Aquavelvet and two-thirds Aquaglaze.

STEP 3. Working in and out of the first glaze color that was applied, cover the other 40 percent of the wall. The second glaze color in this project is one-third Benjamin Moore #1028 Aquavelvet mixed with two-thirds Aquaglaze.

STEP 4. Rag off the glaze colors with a cotton rag. Use a firm hand motion in a hit-skip movement on the wall to create the pattern.

FINISH

Your end product should look something like this.

This two-color rag treatment is usually a great finish for the more casual rooms in your home, but I've seen it work beautifully in formal areas as well.

Apply three different values of the same color with folded cotton rags to create this look. Allow the color to be more opaque or transparent by varying the thickness of the paint left on the surface.

Chapter 3

Waterfall

This is a close-up of the waterfall treatment.

Kathleen, who works with me, named this finish the waterfall because of the soft flowing colors undulating in and out of each other in a vertical pattern. This is an easy faux finish to do and takes very little material to execute it.

PREPARATION

Base coat the walls in a latex low-luster paint. On this job I used Benjamin Moore #641 Aquavelvet as my lightest color. Apply two coats of the paint for 100 percent even coverage. Use your three empty buckets to mix your three colors (one of which is your base coat color) with Aquaglaze. Make up a glaze mixture for each color by using two-thirds Aquaglaze to one-third Aquavelvet.

MATERIALS
- 3 water-based paints
- 3 empty gallon buckets
- 3 paint trays
- 1 9-inch roller handle
- ⅜-inch-nap roller cover
- Cotton rags
- Stir stick
- 2-inch chip brush
- Aquaglaze
- 2-inch blue tape
- Gloves

Pro Tips
✱ Don't overwork areas when blending colors or you will create just one color value.

✱ Use your chip brush around the ceiling and baseboards to continue the pattern from the rags in places the rags can't reach.

✱ Make sure you keep two or three color values on each color as you blend it out.

✱ Apply your first three colors but maintain balance in the composition by adding back in the dark or light colors on a second pass.

STEP 1. Roll a base coat of latex Aquavelvet on wall in two coats using the 9-inch roller handle and ⅜-inch roller cover. Allow to dry.

STEP 2. Fold a cotton cloth into a flat pad that has very few wrinkles on the bottom.

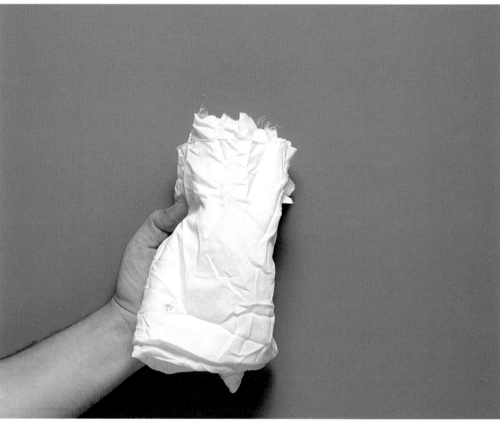

STEP 3. Using your darkest value color, here I used Benjamin Moore #644 Aquavelvet, apply paint to the bottom of pad only. Use a different pad for each color.

STEP 4. In long vertical strokes, cover 60 to 70 percent of the dried base color with your darkest color. You want to establish two or three values of your color. Do this by wiping areas more heavily or more lightly with your glaze color.

STEP 5. In long vertical strokes, apply the mid-value color, for this I used Benjamin Moore #642 Aquavelvet, over 50 to 60 percent of the board overlapping and blending in and out of the darkest color.

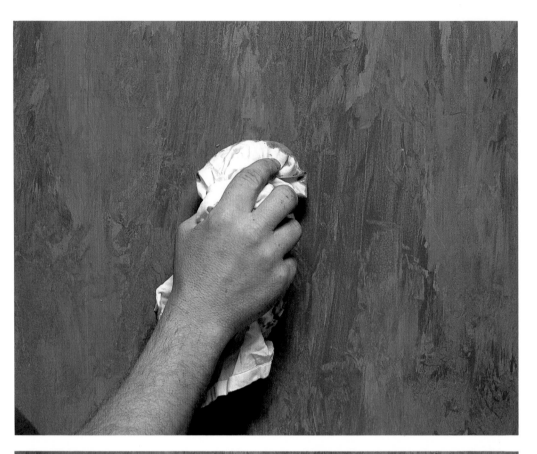

STEP 6. In vertical strokes, apply the lightest color in areas where you wish to create higher contrast in the finish, overlapping in and out of the medium and dark areas. Be careful not to overwork any area and lose your contrast. If you do lose contrast, go back in with the dark or light colors and pump up the contrast where needed.

FINISH
The waterfall's distinct look adds subtle flair to this already beautiful kitchen.

The light stain on the rough-sawed paneling breathes new life into this room. The room is now open and inviting.

Chapter 4

Lightening Up Dark Paneling

This chapter will show you how to take a dark stained wood or processed paneling of years gone by and bring back its beauty by lightening up its color. This will allow you to keep your wonderful wood texture and grain but bring the color tone of the wood into the 1990s and beyond. By lightening up your dark paneling, you will be able to coordinate your room with today's styles, fabrics, tile, carpets, draperies and more. All of this without the extraordinary expense of tearing out the wood and starting from scratch!

If you have dark paneling like the ones shown here, this chapter will show you how to lighten and brighten it to give your room a whole new look.

PREPARATION

First, you need to make sure the surface you are going to work on is free of any dirt, grease or wax buildup. If your surface has any dirt or grease on it, you need to wipe it down with a good cleaning agent that will not leave a residue when dry, such as T.S.P or Soilax. If it is a waxed wood, you need to remove the wax with a wax remover.

Next, you need to use a product like E.S.P., which will change the chemical composition of the varnish or urethane that was originally applied to your wood as a protective coating, so that your new oil-based stain will adhere to the wood. If your surface is rough-sawed wood paneling, you do not need to do this step. Just make sure the surface is dust-free, and then go ahead and stain it.

Now, mix up an oil-based, low-luster paint in an empty 1-gallon bucket. Use 1 quart of paint to ½ to ¾ quart of paint thinner. The exact mix will depend upon how porous your surface is. The less porous, the less thinner you use.

MATERIALS
- A cleaning degreasing agent such as T.S.P.
- E.S.P.
- Paint thinner
- Oil-based low-luster paint
- Cotton rags
- 1 empty gallon bucket
- Stir stick
- 1 2½- or 3-inch oil brush
- 2 3- or 4-inch chip brushes
- 2-inch blue tape
- Gloves

Pro Tips
* Stain only two to four boards at a time and keep a clean edge down your outside groove as you go.
* Avoid working back into finished areas. This can create a "hole" in your finish.
* Pay close attention to any runs or drips in your finish after you have completed an area.
* Use a dry chip brush to help even out your stain around any molding areas.
* Practice on the back side of a door or the underside of a shelf before doing a noticeable area. This will help you verify your color and technique where it will be least noticeable.
* Apply a little stain on the board and work it out to all areas. A thin, even coat is best.
* On rough-sawed wood you can apply a full wet coat of stain because it will soak in. You only need to wipe it off to even out the stain.

STEP 1. First you need to wipe your surface clean of any dirt, grease or wax buildup. Use T.S.P. or Soilax to clean your surface. Then use E.S.P. or its equivalent to soften up the varnish or urethane so you will create a good surface for your stain to bond to.

STEP 2. Using your oil brush, first apply the stain into the grooves with 100 percent coverage.

STEP 3. Even out the stain from the grooves for 100 percent coverage of two to four boards at once. Make sure you keep a clean outside working edge. Keep the stain as even in consistency as possible.

STEP 4. Evenly wipe off the face of your boards. The grooves may appear lighter than the face of the board at this time. The grooves are usually more porous than the face and will accept and retain more glaze color.

STEP 5. Your boards should look like this after you have wiped them off.

STEP 6. Cut back into your outside clean edge with your new wet edge and repeat steps two through four on the next set of boards. Remember to stain no more than two to four boards at a time.

Other Kinds of Paneling

You can lighten up paneling that consists of boards of any color and size. When you decide it's time for a change, try this technique and watch the dramatic makeover it gives your room.

STEP 1. Make sure your rough-sawed paneling is dust-free.

STEP 2. Using your oil brush, first apply the stain into the grooves with 100 percent coverage. Even out the stain from the grooves for 100 percent coverage of two to four boards at once. Make sure you keep a clean outside working edge. Keep the stain as even in consistency as possible.

STEP 3. Fold up a rag so that the part that will touch the boards is as smooth as possible. Evenly wipe off the face of your boards. The grooves may appear lighter than the face of the board at this time. The grooves are usually more porous than the face and will dry with more color. Cut back into your outside clean edge with your new wet edge and repeat steps two and three until you've done all of the boards.

STEP 1. First you need to wipe your surface clean of any dirt, grease or wax buildup. Use T.S.P. or Soilax to clean your surface. Then use E.S.P. or its equivalent to soften up the varnish or urethane so you will create a good surface for your stain to bond to.

STEP 2. Using your oil brush, first apply the stain into the grooves with 100 percent coverage. Even out the stain from the grooves for 100 percent coverage of two to four boards at once. Make sure to keep a clean outside working edge. Keep the stain as even in consistency as possible.

STEP 3. Fold up a rag so that the part that will touch the boards is as smooth as possible. Evenly wipe off the face of your boards. The grooves may appear lighter than the face of the board at this time. The grooves are usually more porous than the face and will dry with more color. Cut back into your outside clean edge with your new wet edge and repeat steps two and three until you've done all of the boards.

Notice the diagonal pattern of the newsprint finish. When trying this technique in your own home, step back from your work periodically to make sure the pattern is consistent.

PHOTOGRAPH BY RON FORTH © 1995

Chapter 5

Newsprint

Newsprint is an easy decorative paint finish to do. I find that using this finish in foyers creates a nice, sophisticated look. I have also used this in master bedrooms, dining rooms, first floor powder baths and family rooms. The diagonal pattern of this treatment tends to open up a room and make it appear larger than it is.

PREPARATION

Apply two coats of your base paint. For this demonstration, I used Benjamin Moore #754 Aquavelvet. Let your base coat dry. You will need to fold up 100-200 sheets of newsprint before you start the room. Also make up your oil-based glaze for the room. A 12′ × 12′ × 8′ room will not take any more than 1 quart of paint (in this case Benjamin Moore #1534 Satin Impervo), 1 quart of Benjamin Moore Alkyd Glazing Liquid and ¾ to 1 quart of paint thinner. Try adding ¾ quart of paint thinner first. If the glaze seems a little thick and the base color doesn't come through, add the rest of the thinner. Also, on really hot days or on large walls, you can add ½ to 1 cup of boiled linseed oil to your mix to increase its drying time.

The newsprint finish is a negative application. You take glaze off your base coat with blank newsprint to create this look.

MATERIALS
- Benjamin Moore #754 Aquavelvet
- Benjamin Moore #1534 Satin Impervo
- 24″ × 36″ blank newsprint
- Roller handle
- Roller cover
- Paint tray
- Cut brush
- Benjamin Moore Alkyd Glazing Liquid
- Paint thinner
- 2-inch blue tape
- Gloves

Pro Tips
- ❋ Pre-fold 100-200 sheets of 24″ × 36″ blank newsprint for a 12′ × 12′ × 8′ room before starting your glazing.
- ❋ Do edges first with a clean edge of newsprint in the area you are glazing, then work into the field of the wall.
- ❋ Run diagonally from top left to bottom right.
- ❋ Maintain the same angle (approximately 45°) throughout application. Stand back and check for consistency as you go.
- ❋ Use a thin, even coat of glaze covering 100 percent of wall surface area you are working in.

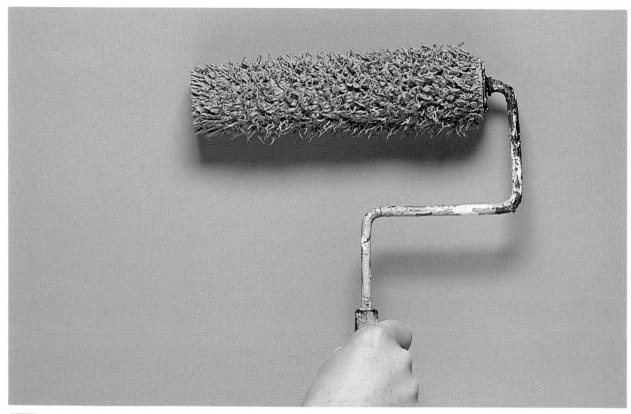

STEP 1. Apply a latex low-luster paint for your base coat. The color shown here is Benjamin Moore #754 Aquavelvet.

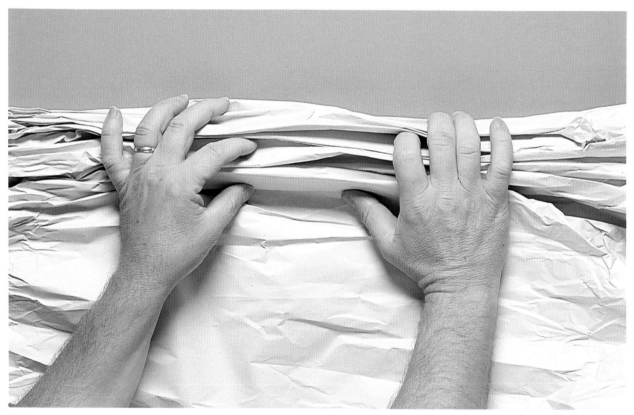

STEP 2. You want to fold the newsprint in an accordion or fan fashion. Make sure you use blank newsprint and not the Sunday paper because the ink will transfer onto the wall. The folds do not have to be any exact size; you just need to put a lot of creases into the paper. I usually fold the 24-inch width of the paper.

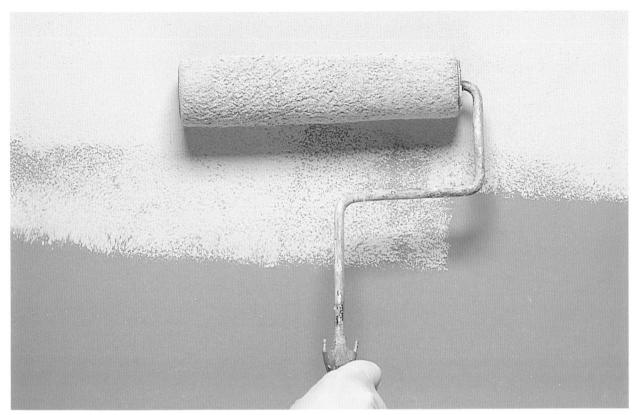

STEP 3. Apply glaze over the blue base coat in a thin, even fashion. Cover 100 percent of the working area.

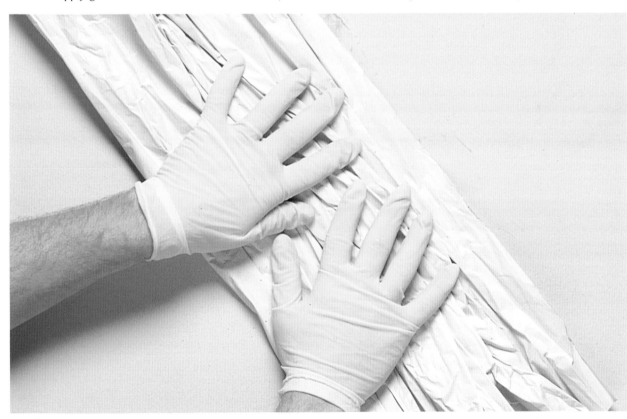

STEP 4. Lay the newsprint down at a 45° angle. I usually start from the top left and work to the lower right.

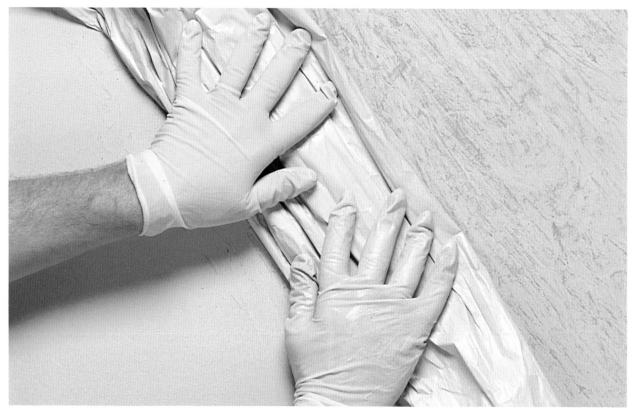

STEP 5. Once the paper is applied where you wish, push the paper down into the glaze. You can work your hand over the paper to flatten it out onto the wall glaze. Fold and unfold the paper until it is saturated with glaze and will not pick up any more glaze from the surface.

STEP 6. Get a new piece of paper if needed. Tie into the existing pattern making sure your angles remain constant.

STEP 7. Avoid this mistake by applying the newsprint in a consistent diagonal fashion.

FINISH

The newsprint technique is quick and easy. You can give your room a whole new, sophisticated look in one afternoon.

This beautiful treatment actually incorporates several techniques: a two-color rag blend (described in chapter two), imprinting and the crackle finish.

Chapter 6

Crackle Finish

If you want one of the prettiest texture treatments going, this is what you need. This chapter actually describes three different treatments. You can have a soft, mottled finish with a hand-painted image, a stencil or a Custom Imprint on top of it. Then to add even more character, apply a clear crackle finish over the top. With an umber stain over the crackle, the treatment will appear to have been on your walls for decades.

PREPARATION

Apply the base coat of Off White Aquabond to your walls and allow it to dry. Do your two-color rag blend as described in chapter two. Use your Benjamin Moore Aquavelvet colors for the two-color rag blend. Allow this to dry and then apply your Imprint Coat. Allow that to dry for one hour before applying your image. Once the image is applied, you can seal over it immediately with 100 percent coverage of Aquaseal. This needs to dry for a minimum of two hours before you apply your coat of clear Aquasize. One hour after applying Aquasize, you can follow with the clear crackle over the top of it. You can brush or roll on the clear crackle. Allow the crackle to dry and then glaze the wall with Aquacreme tinted with a 100 percent acrylic paint such as Aquacolor. Rub the glaze off, and you have a beautiful finish.

This vine is more intricate than the one demonstrated, but it gives you an idea of just how much detail can grace your walls.

MATERIALS
- Off White Aquabond
- Aquaglaze
- Aquasize
- Clear Aquacrackle
- Aquacreme
- Dark Brown, Black and French Red Aquacolor
- Custom Imprint Coat
- Aquaseal
- Original Imprint
- 2-inch blue tape
- 2 Benjamin Moore Aquavelvet colors
- Roller handle
- Roller cover
- Paint tray
- Cotton rags
- 4-inch chip brush
- Burnishing stick
- Gloves
- Respirator (optional)

Pro Tips
- ✽ Image Imprint Coat will stay tacky from one to seventy-two hours after applying.
- ✽ As you burnish down your image, check it as you go to make sure it is transferring completely. Do this by lifting up just one corner at a time.
- ✽ The image is fragile before it is bonded to the surface, so handle carefully.
- ✽ The crackle size will stay sticky from one to twelve hours after being applied.
- ✽ If you want larger cracks, apply two coats of crackle size to the surface. Apply the second coat after the first coat has reached a firm tack.

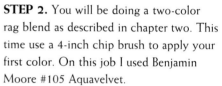

STEP 1. Base coat your walls in Off-White Aquabond.

STEP 2. You will be doing a two-color rag blend as described in chapter two. This time use a 4-inch chip brush to apply your first color. On this job I used Benjamin Moore #105 Aquavelvet.

STEP 3. After applying your first color, add the second color with a different 4-inch chip brush. Shown here is Benjamin Moore #567 Aquavelvet.

STEP 4. Rag off the colors and allow paint to dry.

STEP 5. Apply Custom Imprint Coat. You only need to apply this where you want your image to be. The image will transfer only where the imprint coat is.

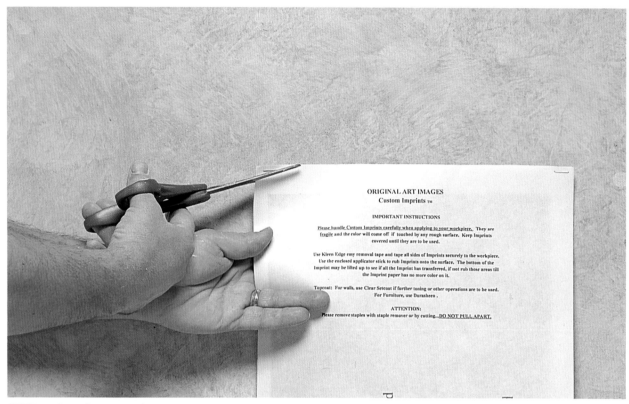

STEP 6. Cut off corners where staples are on the Original Imprint sheets.

STEP 7. Trim away excess paper around your image. You must be careful not to touch the image at this time.

STEP 8. Using blue tape, tape down the edges of the image so it will not move when you start to burnish it. Blue tape has a low-tack adhesive that should do no damage to the surface below. Burnish down the imprint using a flat wood stick. Press firmly over the entire imprint to transfer the image.

STEP 9. Remove paper, checking as you pull it up to make sure the image has transferred. If it hasn't fully transferred, carefully lay the image back down and burnish again.

STEP 10. You can now seal the surface with Aquaseal where you applied the imprint coat. This will neutralize the stickiness of the imprint coat. Allow to dry two hours.

STEP 11. Apply the Aquasize in a 100 percent even coverage of the surface to be crackled. It will only crack where you have the Aquasize. Allow to dry one hour so that the surface remains tacky.

STEP 12. Apply the Clear Aquacrackle using a brush or roller. This material looks milky white when wet but dries clear. Do not overwork this material. Do not disturb it once it is applied. Allow the Aquacrackle to dry thoroughly. The drying time will vary depending on the temperature and the humidity. It will usually dry within two to eight hours. Work only a small area at a time if you plan to bag the surface as described in step 13. The thickness of your Aquacrackle layer will also affect the size of its crackle. A thicker coat creates larger cracks; thinner creates smaller cracks.

STEP 13. If you want to have nondirectional cracks, you can take a piece of plastic and lightly "bag" your surface while it is wet with the Aquacrackle. Do this immediately, because if you wait too long, it will reactivate the size below and the surface will not crack properly.

STEP 14. Tie into your last section completed being careful not to disturb the areas previously done.

STEP 15. Mix your Aquacreme with your Aquacolors. I used Dark Brown, Black, and French Red. Brush or roll the glaze thinly onto the surface.

STEP 16. Take a cotton rag and rub the glaze off the tops of the cracks. This will allow the glaze to stay in the cracks and give the surface a beautiful aged finish.

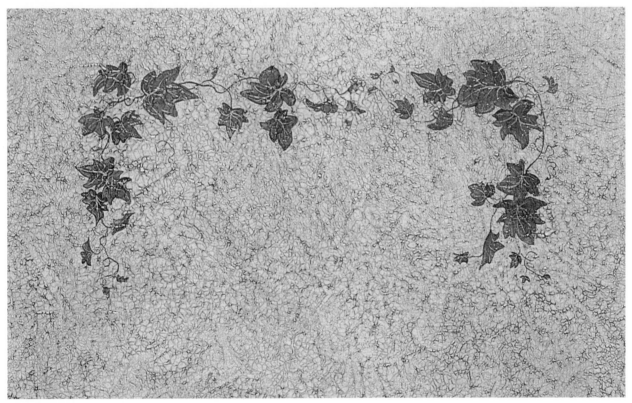

FINISH
Stand back and admire your finished treatment.

The stencils were randomly placed over the tissue paper finish to create the subtle effect shown here.

Chapter 7

Tissue Paper

Affixing tissue paper to a wall is a great treatment that has a leather look. You can also dress the treatment up by adding stripes to it or stenciling over it. It can be used in a formal area such as your foyer or dining room or in a more casual area such as a gathering room or master bedroom. This is also a great finish that can help hide any minor defects in your walls such as scratches, dings, dents, nail pops and cracks, because you apply the tissue directly on top of those areas. Any really bad areas should be repaired prior to applying the tissue, though.

PREPARATION

To prepare for this job you need to crumple up sheets of tissue paper into tight balls and uncrumple them. If you are using a standard size tissue (24″ × 36″), each sheet will cover about five square feet of wall space. So figure your square footage out and divide by five to determine how many sheets you need to do your space. Paper supply dealers will sell a packet of 1,000 sheets of tissue for about $40.

If you wish, you can size your walls with a wallpaper sizing (such as Shields) before applying your tissue. This is not required but would help in removal of the tissue at a later time as well as give you a little more working time while applying the tissue.

To affix the tissue paper, apply either wallpaper heavy-duty clear paste or Elmer's Glue cut 50 percent with water

This is a close-up of stenciling over a tissue paper finish. With a little imagination, you can create an original stencil. Just transfer your artwork to a transparency and cut it out.

MATERIALS
- Tissue paper
- Wallpaper sizing
- Wallpaper paste or Elmer's Glue
- Brush
- Paint tray
- Roller handle
- Roller cover
- Aquaglaze
- Benjamin Moore #1124 Aquavelvet
- Off-White Aquabond
- Cotton rags
- Latex gloves
- 12 photocopies of stencil
- Stencil brush
- 1 transparency of stencil
- X-Acto knife
- Cutting board
- 2-inch blue tape

Pro Tips
- When applying tissue, hold out the edge of the tissue from the molding or ceiling line by about ¹⁄₁₆″ to ⅛″. This makes it easier to demask the trim and ceiling after the project is completed.
- When you come to an area where you do not need a full sheet of paper, you can fold your paper and slightly wet the crease and it will then tear very easily.
- If you have a spot of tissue you don't like on the wall, just cut it out, apply a little paste on the patch area and apply new tissue.
- In corners, it is best to run a straight edge of the sheet of tissue down each side.
- Make a transparency of your original art to use as a stencil.
- Make photocopies of the original art to help establish your pattern.

to your walls. Apply your tissue on top of the adhesive and let it dry for twenty-four hours, and then base coat it with a latex low-luster paint. Allow to dry for two hours, and then you can glaze it with the color of choice. For extra beauty, you can add a stencil or striping pattern on top of your glazed tissue.

STEP 1. Wad tissue paper into a ball and uncrumple it for installation.

STEP 2. Use either a heavy-duty clear wall-paper paste or Elmer's Glue cut 50 percent with water. Apply paste to a wall area that is a little larger than two sheets.

STEP 3. Unfold tissue, hold it by the top two corners and tack it lightly into the paste. Pull down lightly and touch the bottom two edges to the wall so the paper is fairly straight. Smooth out the face of the tissue into the glue with your hand, a brush or a roller. Make sure creases remain and you don't smooth them all out. Push the material in towards itself for more crease.

STEP 4. To join pieces of tissue paper, you will need to apply more paste to the wall and on about one inch of the tissue paper already on the wall.

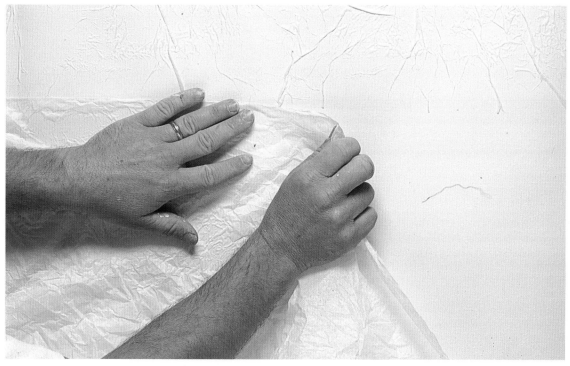

STEP 5. Apply your next piece of tissue paper as you did in step 3. Make sure it overlaps the former pieces by one inch or so.

STEP 6. Roll base coat over the top of the tissue after it has been installed twenty-four hours. Use a latex low-luster paint for your base coat, and paint as you would any ordinary drywall. For this job I used Off-White Aquabond. Make sure the paint goes under any tissue flaps.

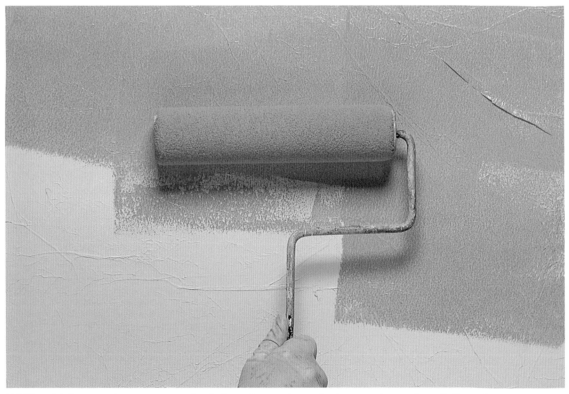

STEP 7. Make up a glaze using two-thirds Aquaglaze and one-third #1124 Aquavelvet. Roll on glaze in sections at a time. Allow to dry.

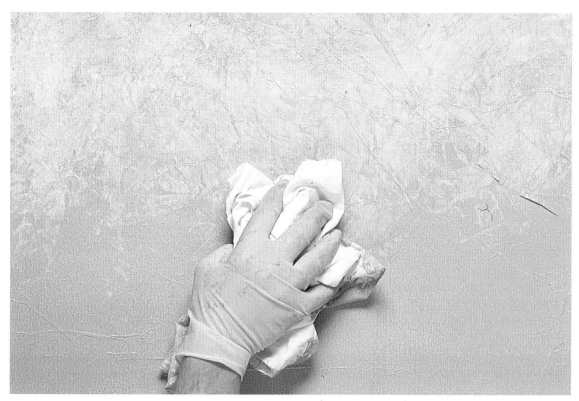

STEP 8. Rag off glaze using cotton rags. Partially rub off the glaze and push it in and around the creases.

STEP 9. Once the glaze is dry you can stencil over it. Make twelve photocopies of your stencil design and cut them out of the paper. Using a piece of tape, tape the patterns to your wall in a random design. This will enable you to check out your placement before you begin stenciling.

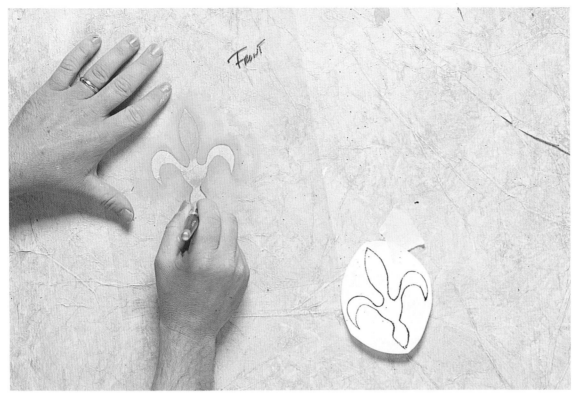

STEP 10. Stencil in the design using the exact color you used for your glazing color, except use it straight from the Aquavelvet can with no glaze in it.

FINISH

You can make a stencil from a design you already have in the room or from your imagination. You can also buy ready-made stencils from your local paint and craft stores.

This beautiful Tissue Paper finish can be removed at a later date. If you use wallpaper sizing before you begin papering, removal goes much more quickly.

Changing the colors you use for your torn-paper finish can significantly alter the look of this treatment.

Chapter 8

Torn Paper

Torn paper is a very popular finish around the country now and it can be done by moderately skilled artisans. This is a beautiful finish that can give you a wide variety of looks. It is also a good treatment to be used over walls that have minor damage because it helps to hide the flaws.

You can also apply torn paper over existing wallpaper, but if you do, your substrate wallpaper needs to be securely fastened to the wall. You will also need to size the old wallpaper with a product like Shields before applying the torn paper. You need to be aware, however, that even though I have done this with success, I cannot guarantee that the paper will stay up because of the extra weight of the new torn paper on top of the old wallpaper.

PREPARATION

It is easiest to paint the kraft paper decorative paint finish in long strips of 4-foot-wide paper. I can do two or three 20-foot-long strips on my garage floor. I first lay plastic or canvas drop cloths on the concrete and then lay out three strips of paper so I can walk in between them.

I put my paint roller on the pole extension and paint the kraft paper while standing up. For this job I used Benjamin Moore #1027 Aquavelvet. I let this dry and then glaze it with a mixture of one-third Benjamin Moore #1214 Aquavelvet and two-thirds Aquaglaze. I roll this glaze on the same way, covering 90 to

MATERIALS
- 60 lb. kraft paper—3 or 4 feet wide on a roll or in 24″ × 36″ sheets
- Benjamin Moore #1027 Aquavelvet
- Benjamin Moore #1214 Aquavelvet
- Aquaglaze
- Cellulose sponge
- Gold metallic spray paint or gold metallic paint
- Heavy-duty clear wallpaper paste
- Wallpaper smoothing tool
- Paint roller
- Paint roller cover
- Paint tray
- Wallpaper razor blade tool
- Cotton rags
- Pole extension
- Platic or canvas drop cloths
- Shields wallpaper sizing
- 2-inch blue tape
- Gloves

100 percent of the paper, and pat it off with the cellulose sponge. Once this is dry, I spray on an uneven light spray of gold metallic paint. I then tear up the paper and apply it with wallpaper paste to walls that have been sized with a wallpaper sizing.

For this treatment, you actually make your own wallpaper and then hang it in torn sheets.

Pro Tips
- ❋ Work on as large a sheet of kraft paper as possible.
- ❋ You will need 50 percent more square feet of painted paper than you have square feet of wall space to cover.
- ❋ Tear paper in a slicing fashion.
- ❋ Do not tear in triangles or square shapes. Go for soft amorphic shapes that are eight to eighteen inches in size.
- ❋ Save some small pieces for patching.
- ❋ If you don't like to hang wallpaper or do not know how to hang it, hire a professional paperhanger.
- ❋ Use a wallpaper smoothing tool to even out paper.
- ❋ Use a wallpaper razor blade to trim excess paper around windows, baseboards, ceilings and so on.

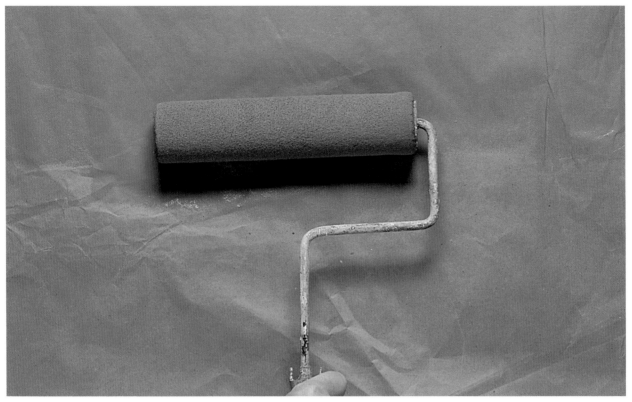

STEP 1. Working with as large a piece of kraft paper as is manageable, apply your base coat. In this case, I used Benjamin Moore #1027 Aquavelvet.

STEP 2. Roll on glaze with 90 to 100 percent coverage of your paper strip.

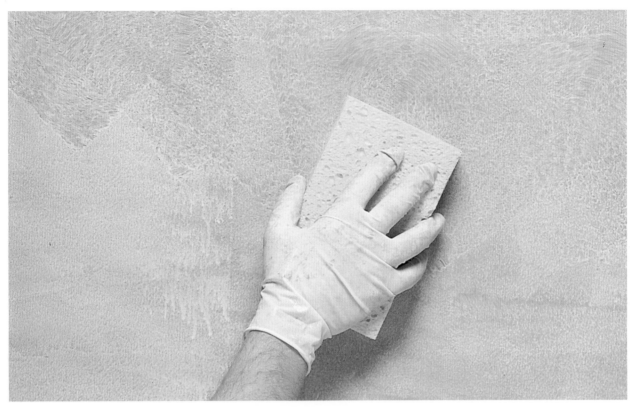

STEP 3. Use a cellulose sponge to break up the glaze color and create a nice soft, broken-color technique. When using the sponge, pat the surface firmly using a slight twisting-sliding motion. Let dry completely.

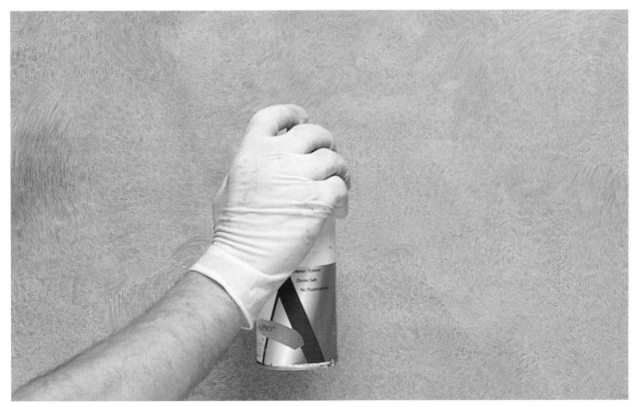

STEP 4. Use a gold metallic spray paint and hold it six to twelve inches from the surface. Give a light dusting of gold over the surface. Move your hand quickly as you spray to avoid any heavy concentration of gold in one area. It is desirable to have a slightly mottled look, so do not spray the entire surface area. Cover maybe sixty to eighty percent and let dry. As an option, apply any gold metallic paint in a positive application method using either a sponge, feather duster or a rag as your tool.

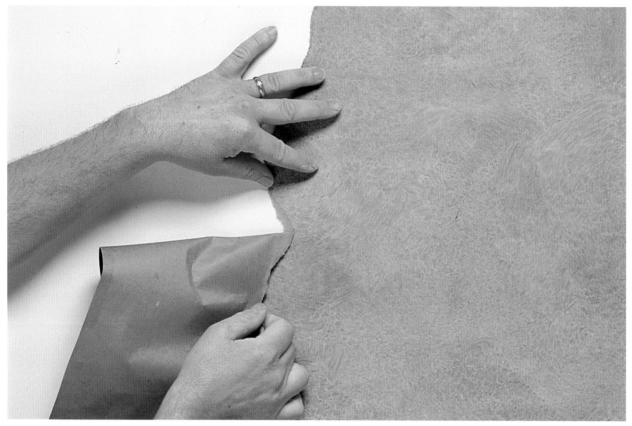

STEP 5. When tearing the paper, slice it back in on itself to allow the edge of kraft paper to show.

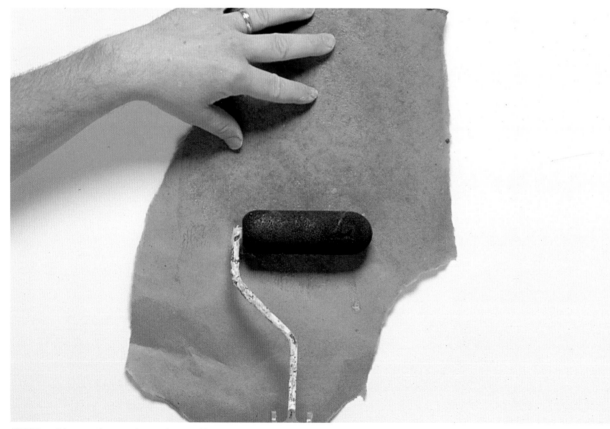

STEP 6. Using a heavy-duty, clear wallpaper paste, paste the back of each piece of paper and let it sit for one to two minutes before applying to the wall. You can do four or five pieces at once.

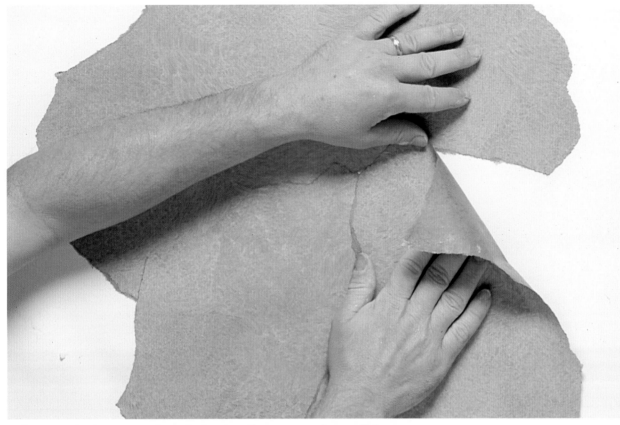

STEP 7. Apply the paper to the wall. Overlap all pieces so no bare wall shows.

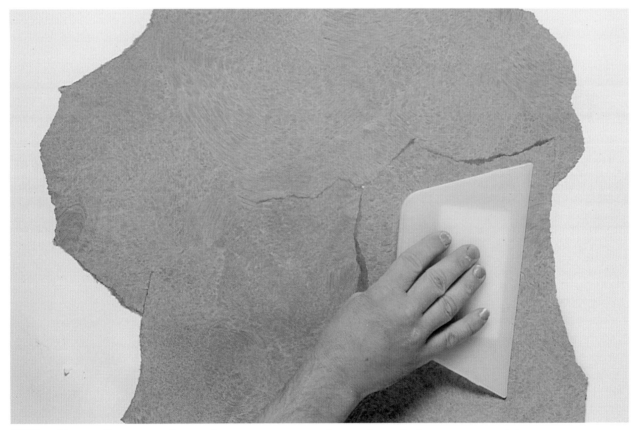

STEP 8. Use a wallpaper smoothing tool to move excess paste from underneath the paper to smooth it out.

STEP 9. Keep a clean work area as you go. Wipe off your pasting table as well as the face of each piece of installed paper using water on a clean cellulose sponge. Then use a dry rag to wipe off the face of the wet paper.

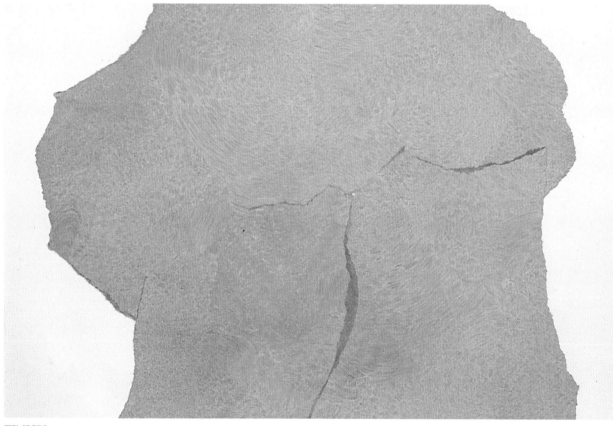

FINISH

You have just hung hand-painted wallpaper.

The subtle colors used in this finish add just the right amount of drama to the master bedroom.

The faux stone finish makes this guy feel right at home.

PHOTOGRAPH BY JOE VAN DE HATERT AND LANIER PRATT OF AUDIBLE ELEGANCE

Chapter 9

Stone Block

Dimensional texture finishes are becoming increasingly popular. Combine that fact with how "hot" Old World distressed techniques are, and you have one of today's most sought-after finishes. A lot of restaurants and commercial properties are using these finishes. Also high-end residential clients will seek the finish to be used in foyers, media rooms, bathrooms and studies.

PREPARATION

Base coat the walls in any of the Aquabond base colors. I used Off-White for this job. Decide on the sizes of your blocks, and then lay up your pattern. The pattern I used here is similar to that used in Warwick Castle, an English castle built in the 1400s. It is a good idea to work from photographs or from books that show how real stone masons lay up different patterns.

This is just one kind of stone look you can create with this finish. Let your eyes wander to come up with a style that works for you.

MATERIALS

- Snap string
- Measuring tape
- Level
- 2-inch masking tape
- Squirrel mixer
- Roller handle
- Roller cover
- Paint tray
- 6- and 8-inch-wide drywall blades
- Aquabond
- Aquastone
- Aquacreme
- Aquacolor
- Cotton rags
- 120-grit sandpaper
- 2- and 4-inch chip brushes
- Latex gloves
- #4 Pencil
- 2-inch blue tape

Pro Tips

- ❋ Use snap string to connect your long points for your pattern.
- ❋ Mix baby powder fifty-fifty with blue chalk in your chalk box. Chalk marks are easier to remove later.
- ❋ When tearing tape, apply the tape to the wall first and then tear the edges on both sides of the tape to create your ragged grout line.
- ❋ For a more free-form approach to your block, you can trowel on the Aquastone and create the blocks with no tape for the grout.
- ❋ Remove tape while stone is still wet but a little tacked up, anywhere from one half to one, hour depending on drying conditions.
- ❋ Look at real stone block buildings for composition of the stone.
- ❋ If you wish to have your colors soak into the Aquastone more fully and be more translucent, you can add up to 30 percent water to the Aquacreme.

STEP 1. Apply Off-White Aquabond base coat.

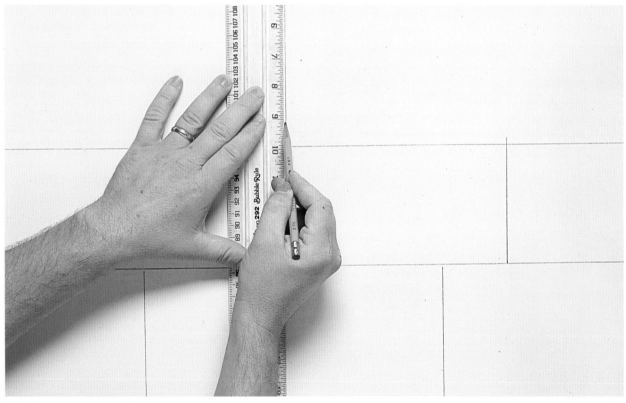

STEP 2. Use a pencil and snap string to lay up your pattern. Make sure you check your lines both vertically and horizontally so they are level and plumb. On smaller walls where you can use a level you can connect the dots with a pencil. Use a #4 pencil so the lines are light and easy to cover up later.

STEP 3. For the grout pattern, apply 2-inch masking tape over the lines. Tear the tape on the top and bottom edge making sure to leave tape in varying thicknesses everywhere that you want to have grout.

STEP 4. Mix the Aquastone with 10 to 20 percent water using a squirrel mixer (or other type). Apply mixture to 100 percent of the area right on top of the tape. Either expose an edge of the tape now or extend the edge of the tape onto the baseboard or ceiling line so you can find it later to remove it. Lay the material on in varying thicknesses, keeping the depth between one-sixth to one-half inch. When troweling it on, push and move the material, creating varying textures. I usually pull the material in one direction for each block.

STEP 5. Remove the tape after one-half to one hour drying time. The material should have started to get a dry shine on top but still be soft and pliable underneath.

STEP 6. I used Aquacreme tinted with Aquacolors Dark Brown, Black and White. I created three different values with these colors and applied them one at a time onto each individual block with a 4-inch chip brush. I wanted some blocks darker and others lighter. Look for a good balance for your composition. Also, think about your light source at this time to help start establishing your shadows.

STEP 7. Apply the mid-value color, working wet into your first glaze color.

STEP 8. Apply the brightest-value color, working it into any unpainted areas and blending wet into wet with values one and two. Rub off glaze with a cotton rag, removing any excess paint at this time. This is where you can check and correct your color balance by wiping off more or less glaze.

STEP 9. Take your darkest value of color and dilute it with 30 percent water. Then take a 2-inch chip brush and drag the color onto the bottom of each stone block and onto one side. Allow the color to go onto the stone and into your grout. Soften out these areas with a rag so the shadow will appear natural.

STEP 10. Using your darkest color from step 9 and a 2-inch chip brush, drag the color up into the bottom edge of your stone so that the color will run downward. You may even use some of the mid-value color this way. When the stone is dry, use a piece of 120-grit sandpaper to sand across the raised area of the stone. This will help increase your highlights and give an extra dimension to your project.

FINISH

You will change the feel of your entire room with this distressed stone finish. Of course, even this stone finish can have a polished look by varying the colors used and by making the stones more uniform in size.

The sand drift finish shown here wonderfully complements many decors.
It is at home among contemporary furnishings and antiques.

Chapter 10

Sand Drifts

Textured finishes are very popular right now, but a lot of people are a little hesitant to have a permanent texture applied to their walls. If you are wary of a permanent textured finish, this treatment may be the right one for you.

It has the look and depth of a dimensional textured finish but it is flat to the touch. For this job, we wanted a neutral color wall finish with a contemporary yet Old World sort of feel to it. This finish worked perfectly.

PREPARATION

To work with the material correctly, you have to get your timing right. If you go too slow, the sand drifts will not develop because the material will dry hard before you move it. If you go too fast, you will blur out your pattern because it is too wet. Look for areas where the Aquatex has already started to dry and then move the wet areas into the drier areas to develop the pattern.

This versatile finish looks like it has a rough texture yet it is nearly flat to the touch.

This is a squirrel mixer.

MATERIALS
- Off-White Aquabond
- Aquatex
- Dark Brown Aquacolor
- Squirrel mixer
- ½-inch drill
- Empty gallon bucket
- Roller handle
- Roller cover
- Paint tray
- 2½-inch brush
- 4-inch chip brush
- Terry cloth towel
- 2-inch blue tape
- Cardboard
- Gloves

Pro Tips

✽ Mix Aquatex with the squirrel mixer attached to your ½-inch drill. At this time you can add 100 percent acrylic colorant and up to 20 percent water to thin the material if desired.

✽ Roll the glaze on evenly with the outside edges being in an uneven random pattern. Remember to roll your glaze as tight as possible into your cut lines (created when you use your 2½-inch brush to cut in).

✽ Soften the outside edges first with your dampened terry cloth towel. Then rag the inside.

✽ Use short, whisper-soft strokes at first. Make two or three passes over your working area allowing the material to develop the sand drifts slowly.

✽ As the material dries, use firmer, longer strokes to move the wet material into the drier areas. This creates the sand drift movement.

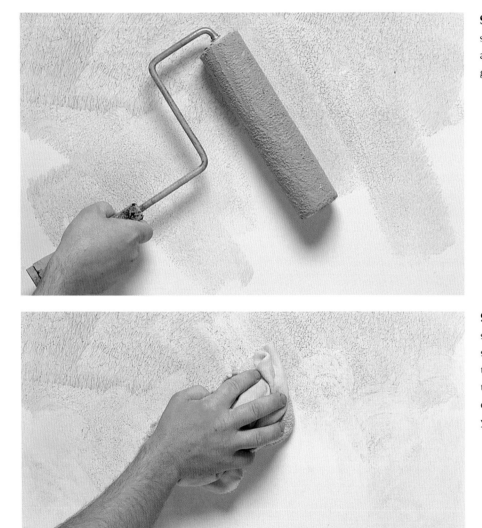

STEP 1. Base coat surface with Off-White Aquabond.

STEP 2. Roll on Aquatex in a two to three-square-foot area. Make sure the coat is even, and leave the outside edge in a random jagged pattern.

STEP 3. Your terry cloth towel should be slightly damp with water. Use the towel to soften the outside edge first. Fade the Aquatex paint into the dry Aquabond base coat; then pat off the inside areas with the terry cloth towel, leaving high and low spots in your glaze.

STEP 4. Hold the 4-inch brush perpendicular to the surface and start to brush the lower glazed areas first with a whisper-soft, short stroke. Work the outside edge first and move into the center.

STEP 5. You will usually need two short, soft passes first and then you can move in a harder, longer brushstroke as the material starts to develop sand drifts. Move the Aquatex material mostly in the same direction that you started in. If you go completely back across the direction you started in, you run the risk of wiping out the pattern.

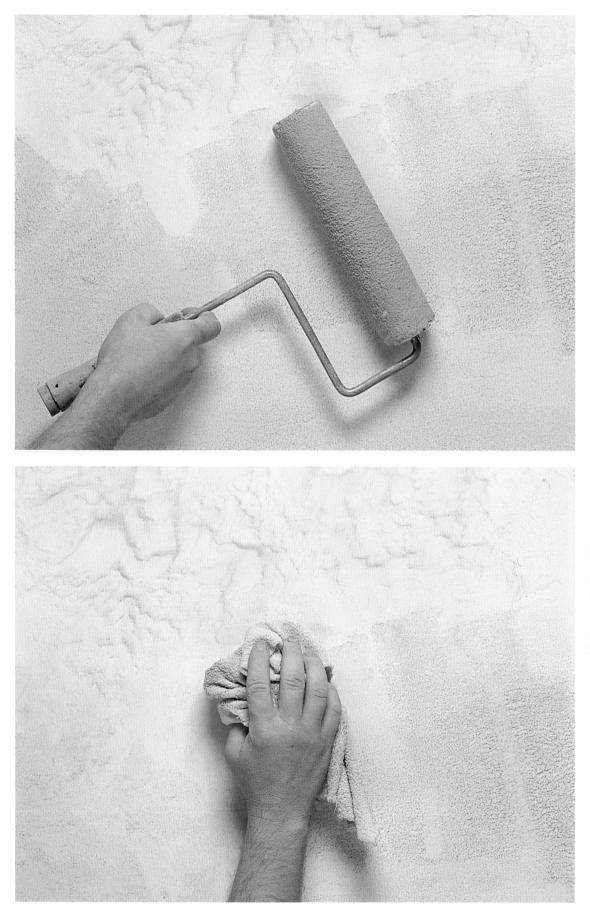

STEP 6. To connect sections to complete a wall, roll on the Aquatex as before but keep it about one-half to one inch away from the area you just completed.

STEP 7. Pat off the material with a damp terry cloth towel working your outside edge and then fade it into your just completed dry finished area. Pat off the center area and fade out your edges.

STEP 8. Brush out the Aquatex the same as before.

STEP 9. If you wish to add more dimension to your project, take a piece of cardboard and tear it in an irregular shape. Lay the cardboard on the surface and brush or spray the Aquatex into its ragged edge.

STEP 10. Remove the cardboard and soften the outside edge into the dry Aquatex.

FINISH

Instead of using a brush to create this ridge line, you can also spray the Aquatex over the cardboard using a High-Volume, Low-Pressure (HVLP) sprayer.

Sand Drift creates the illusion of a coarse texture by depositing color in this sweeping fashion.

The walls in this ornate dining room get their texture from the application of a mixture of latex paint with drywall compound.

Chapter 11
Metallic Textured Finish

In this dining room the designer wanted to have an elegant, contemporary textured finish. The colors were keyed off the custom rug and the chair fabric. We decided to use an antiqued silver metallic base coat for its elegance. We also did a hand-painted stencil border in a metallic gold paint on top of a mottled background. The ceiling, where we used 23K gold leaf squares in between the painted beams, was the crowning glory of the room.

Only a small percentage of the Antique Silver Metallic Aquabond base coat shows through the colors brushed on over it.

PREPARATION

After the room is prepped, base coat your walls and let them dry. For this job, I used Antique Silver Metallic Aquabond. Get two empty gallon-size containers. Mix together one of your flat latex paint colors with drywall compound using your drill and squirrel mixer. The mixture should be about 60 percent paint and 40 percent drywall compound. Mix your second color in the same ratio as the first. The drywall compound affects the color you mix into it. The more compound you mix in, the lighter the color will be.

MATERIALS
- Antique Silver Metallic Aquabond
- Roller handle
- Roller cover
- 2 paint trays
- 3 2½-inch angled brushes
- Drywall compound
- Benjamin Moore #1167 Regal Wall Satin flat latex
- Benjamin Moore #1149 Regal Wall Satin flat latex
- Squirrel mixer
- Drill
- 2 empty gallon containers
- 2-inch blue tape
- Gloves

Pro Tips
- ❋ Blend colors wet into wet in a vertical pattern.
- ❋ Leave about 5 percent of your base coat color showing through the other colors.
- ❋ Use older brushes for this technique. It looks better plus it doesn't ruin your good brushes.
- ❋ Check your vertical pattern for consistency as you go.

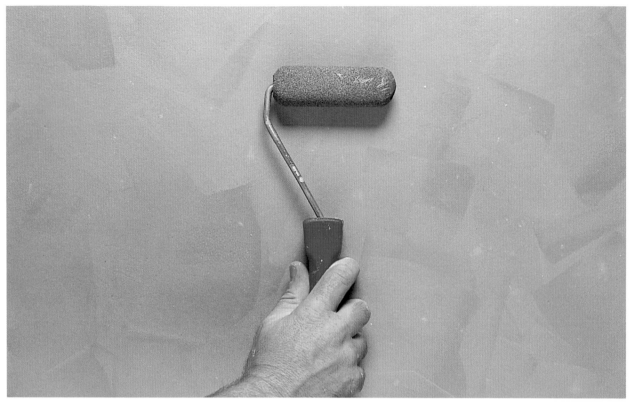

STEP 1. Roll on the base coat and let it dry. (Use a 9-inch roller for this base coat. I used this small roller strictly for demonstration purposes.)

STEP 2. Hold your loaded brush flat against the wall in a vertical hit-skip motion. This will create your pattern of texture—raised more in some areas and lower in others.

STEP 3. Apply your first color covering about 70 to 80 percent of the surface. For this job, I used Benjamin Moore #1167 Regal Wall Satin.

STEP 4. Apply your second color covering about 60 to 70 percent of the surface, blending the two colors together while wet. In this picture, I am using Benjamin Moore #1149 Regal Wall Satin.

STEP 5. To show tie-in of painted areas, take your first color and pat it into the just-finished area in a section of about 2′ × 3′.

STEP 6. Do the same thing with your second color.

The furnishings and paint finish in this dining room make use of a precious metals theme.

This classically elegant paint finish never loses its appeal.

Photographed by Ron Forth © 1995

Chapter 12

Wall Striping

Striping is a classic and elegant way to decorate. It is timeless in its style, not subject to being in or out of fashion. Striping is well-suited for almost any room in the house. It looks great in a dining room, kitchen, foyer, master bedroom, bathrooms and more. It is perhaps one of the most frequently used of all painted decorating styles because it can be coordinated with everything and is very easy to do.

PREPARATION

Base coat the walls in a latex semigloss paint. You want this paint to cover 100 percent of the surface area with two coats of paint for even coverage. Decide on how wide you want your stripes—1″, 4″, 6″, 8″, 12″ or whatever. In the photo the stripes are 4″ wide. Remember, if you do a 2″-wide pattern you will have twice as many stripes to do as you would for a 4″-wide pattern.

When laying out your pattern in a room, start out in your least obvious corner. Behind the door coming into the room is a good place. Using your jig, start to take your pattern around the room stopping when you come to your last wall. It is unlikely that the measurements will fall exactly right into the corner where you started. To compensate for this difference, measure the last wall (from your last completed stripe to the final corner) and divide that measurement by the width of your stripe. The result will probably have a decimal remainder, indicating a certain number of whole stripes plus a fraction of a single stripe left over. Multiply the decimal portion of the number by the original stripe width and then divide that result by the whole portion. Add the resulting fraction to the original stripe width. Use this new, adjusted stripe width for the last wall. Now the stripes will be the same width and there will be no fraction left over at the last corner.

The striping you see is achieved by applying stripes of flat latex paint over the semigloss latex base coat.

MATERIALS
- Roller pan
- Roller handle
- ⅜-inch roller cover
- 2½-inch single brush
- Pencil
- Ruler
- Yardstick
- Low tack adhesive tape
- Level
- Snap string box
- Latex flat paint
- Latex semigloss paint
- Burnishing tool
- 2-inch masking tape
- Gloves

Pro Tips
- Apply the semigloss latex for your base coat and the flat latex for your striping pattern.
- Make a jig to lay up your pattern.
- Use baby powder in your chalk box. It cleans up very well. (Mix with blue chalk for light-colored walls.)
- Check your lines periodically to make sure your striping is level.
- Use a burnishing tool and rub it both ways on the tape to seal it.
- Peel tape away from freshly painted areas to avoid any possible peeling.
- Never use red or yellow chalk on walls. It is permanent.

STEP 1. Use a latex semigloss paint for your base coat when doing a striping finish. This allows your tape to stick better and release better than a flat latex paint. You can also clean up any leftover chalk lines more easily.

STEP 2. To make a jig, I use a low-tack adhesive tape called Easy Mask. I put two pieces of tape side by side and mark one "top" and one "bottom." I then take a pencil and a ruler and mark out my striping pattern onto both pieces of tape. I make my tape jig about four to six feet in length. Anything larger than that gets too difficult to manage.

STEP 3. Starting in my least obvious corner of the room, I take my bottom jig and apply it to the baseboard with my far left dot in the corner. I then take my top jig and apply it to the wall about two to three inches down from the ceiling. The far left dot on the jig goes in the corner. I now use my snap string box that has been filled with baby powder. (If I have a light-colored wall, I mix blue chalk with the baby powder so I can see it.) I will snap a line between the top and bottom tape on the first dot out from the corner. I let my chalk line go up to the ceiling over my tape jig.

STEP 4. I now use my level and check to make sure my line is level and plumb. I will correct my tape at this point if necessary. After about every dozen or so lines, I check again to make sure I am staying level. For above doors and windows, you can buy a small level that will fit in these spaces. Once I am at the end of my jig, I remove the tape and start the process all over, lining up my first dot on the last line snapped.

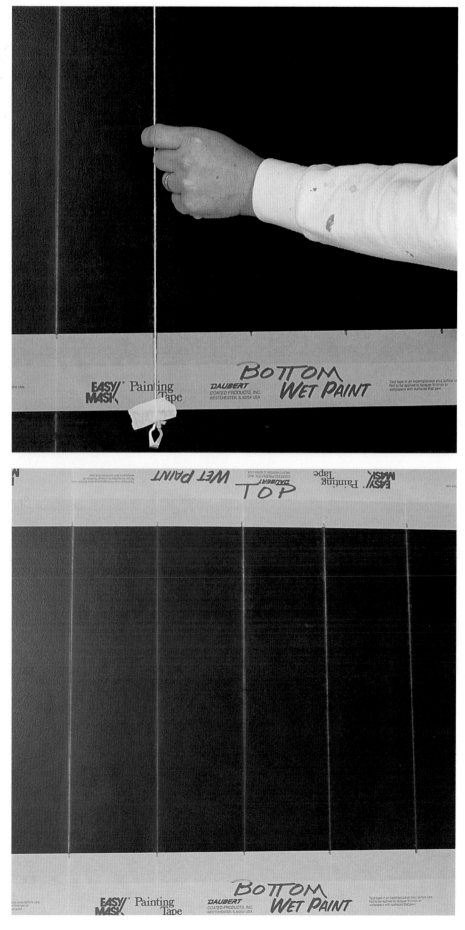

STEP 5. Once I have my pattern snapped all the way around the room, I will use my Easy Mask tape and tape out my pattern. When taping, make sure that you tape on the outside of your chalk line. That way when you paint, it will cover up all of your snap lines and you won't have to wipe any off. Tape out one whole wall.

STEP 6. I tape out one wall and then burnish it with a burnishing tool (a credit card works also). Make sure you burnish both up and down so it seals the tape well to the wall. Test this first so you can determine if removing your burnished tape will peel up or pull off the base coat of paint. If removing the tape does harm your base coat, allow your paint to cure longer and apply less pressure when burnishing.

STEP 7. Now take your flat latex paint in the same color as your semigloss paint and paint it right over the tape. Cover 100 percent of the area with paint. One coat should be fine but be careful to cover the area completely because you will have a sheen contrast wherever you don't.

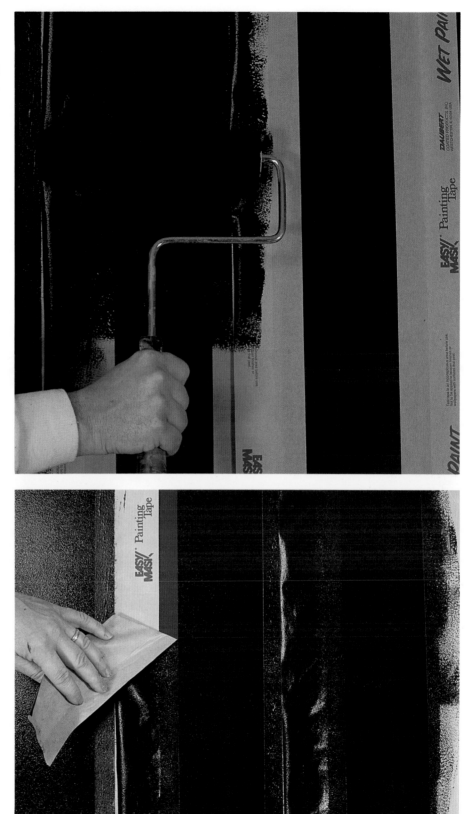

STEP 8. Peel up your tape as soon as you paint the wall. When peeling up the tape, peel it at an angle away from the freshly painted area. This will help avoid peel-ups into the fresh paint.

FINISH

This look is classic and relatively simple to create. All you need to succeed is adequate pre-planning and ample time to execute.

at right

The striping in this dining room was done in the same manner as the project in this chapter. The dining room in this picture has an added leather-like appearance created with the tissue paper technique described in chapter seven.

The short, curved strokes of a rubber comb created the pattern you see on this powder room wall.

C h a p t e r 13

Combing

This is a fast and easy treatment to do and has a beautiful transitional designer-look when completed. I have executed this design in master bedrooms, formal powder baths, merchandising areas in department stores and in kitchens. The extra use of the metallic overglaze in this finish is what sets it apart from the average combed look. It adds an extra warmth and patina to your finish that is very much in demand today.

PREPARATION

Start out by base coating your walls with two coats of Off-White Aquabond. Once this has dried completely, you can mix up the three Aquacolors with the Aquacreme using the squirrel mixer to do so. Roll the Aquacreme mixture on the wall with your roller in 3′ × 3′ sections. Use your rubber triangle comb to create your pattern. Repeat this process until the room is completed. Once it is all dry, you can rub on your metallic overglaze to create a beautiful patina finish.

MATERIALS
- Aquabond Off-White
- Aquacreme
- Aquacolor French Red
- Aquacolor Black
- Aquacolor Dark Brown
- Aquacolor Bronze
- Aquacolor Gold
- Rubber triangle comb
- Cotton rags
- Roller brushes
- 2-inch blue tape
- Paint tray
- Cut bucket
- Squirrel mixer
- Cordless or electric drill
- Gloves

You do not have to glaze over the dried combing though it adds visual interest and character to the finish. This is a close-up of combing with no overglaze.

Pro Tips
- Use squirrel mixer attached to your drill to mix your paints.
- Use the wide tooth in your rubber comb for larger definition of pattern.
- Use a rag to clean the teeth in your comb often.
- When working in corners, next to trim or at the ceiling line, work your comb out from these areas first and then tie it back into the wall area.
- Make sure the Aquacreme is completely dry before overglazing. Pay particular attention in corners where there may be a larger buildup of material.
- Try to always start at the ceiling line with your treatment and work down to the baseboard before you move across the area. This will avoid drips going into finished areas below your work area.
- Roll glaze on evenly with 100 percent coverage. You don't want one area to look like it has more glaze than another.
- When you are mixing your Aquacolors into your Aquacreme, the color will appear darker in the bucket than it will on the wall. Test it out on a board that has your background color on it before applying it to your wall.

STEP 1. Apply two base coats of Aquabond Off-White.

STEP 2. Apply the glaze which has been made of Aquacreme and Aquacolors of your choice. For this job, I used Dark Brown, French Red and Black. Be sure you make up enough glaze for the project in the beginning so that you don't have to re-tint. When tinting Aquacreme with Aquacolor, you don't want the mixture to be more than 30-40 percent Aquacolor. Remember the less Aquacolor into the Aquacreme, the more translucent your color; the more colorant you use, the more opaque and dark your color becomes. A gallon of Aquacreme will do 400-square-feet of wall space. On a wall surface, I would use a 9-inch roller with a ⅜-inch nap cover for this step.

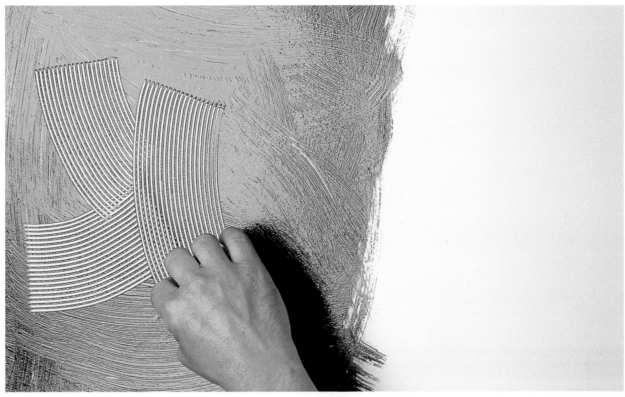

STEP 3. Take your rubber triangle comb and hold it at a 70° to 90° angle to the wall. Pull it through your glaze. Slightly overlap areas so there is no glazing area untouched.

STEP 4. Repeat combing process over larger area. Clean your comb with a rag between strokes as you go.

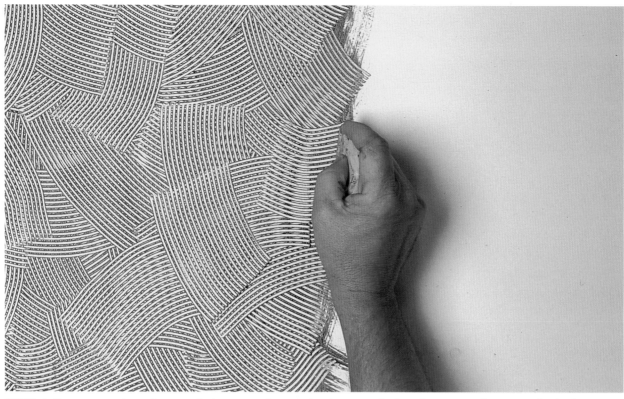

STEP 5. Continue combing, leaving a little area on the outside edge uncombed so that you can bring your fresh glaze into the old.

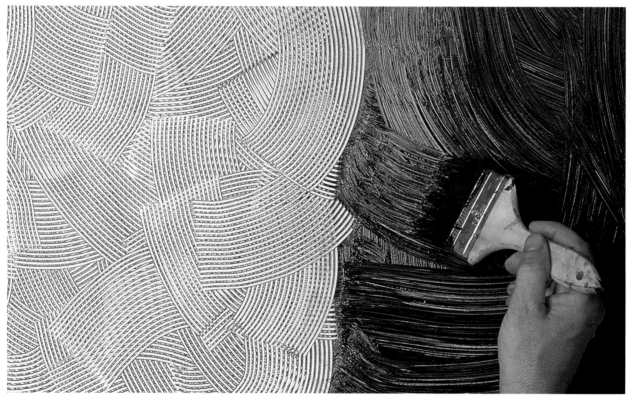

STEP 6. Take fresh glaze and do another section while tying into a combed area.

STEP 7. Start combing your new area by working into the old. Finish out areas and repeat process until the room is complete.

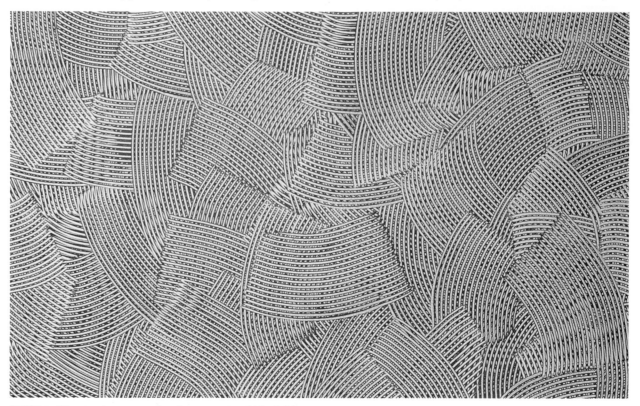

STEP 8. This is what a completed section should look like.

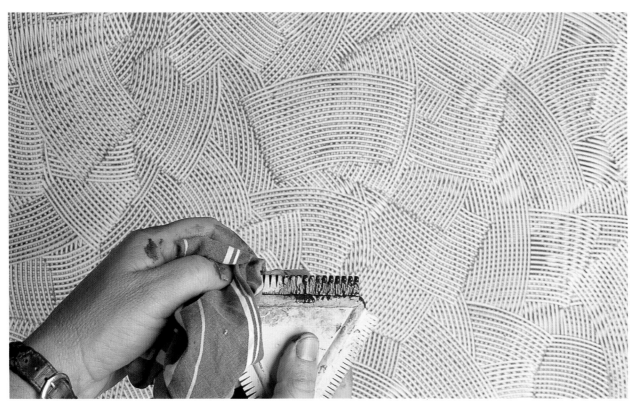

STEP 9. You need to clean the teeth of the comb often. They get clogged up with glaze easily.

STEP 10. Make up a glaze using Aquacreme mixed with a blend of three parts Aquacolor Bronze and two parts Aquacolor Gold. Mix thoroughly with your squirrel mixer and drill. Apply the glaze with a rag.

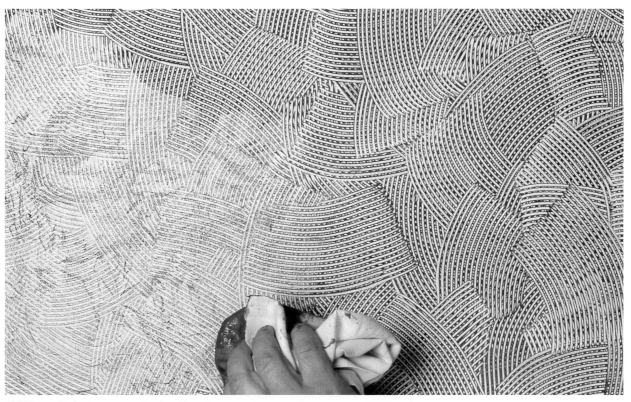

STEP 11. Rub glaze onto the dried combing in a large swirling motion. Be sure to cover 100 percent of the area with an even application of glaze.

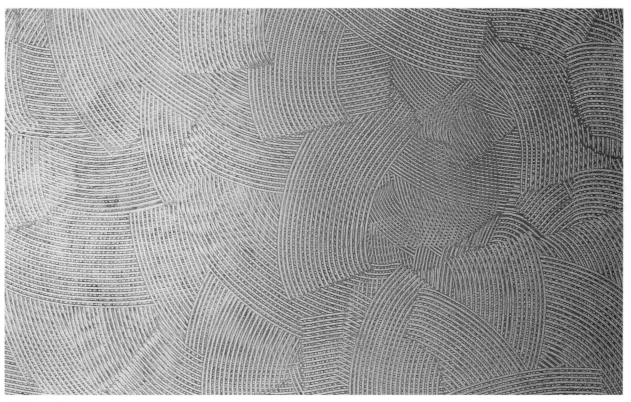

STEP 12. Rub the glaze into a small area. Once it is evenly spread, begin a new section.

Part 3

A Gallery of Gorgeous Finishes

The pictures in this gallery are full-room shots of the projects in this book. They are here as reference material to help you decide what finishes will work best in your home. You can often get great ideas from seeing how professional decorators appoint a room.

The Torn Paper finish pictured in this boudoir was achieved by painting long sheets of kraft paper and tearing them into small, irregular pieces. These pieces are then affixed to the wall with wallpaper paste. To learn more about creating this finish, see chaper eight.

at right
Though this Sand Drift finish looks textured, it is flat to the touch.
Follow the steps in chapter ten to achieve this look.

A clear Crackle Finish with an umber stain over it can give even the newest home an Old World feel.
For information on Custom Imprints and the Crackle Finish, see chapter six.

at left
Metalic finishes are very popular. Notice the dramatic affect that
the combination of metallic paint and the combing finish here on
this powder room. Go to chapter thirteen to find the step-by-step
instructions for creating this finish.

Chapter four gives you step-by-step instructions on how to lighten up dark paneling.
The painted rough-sawed cedar pictured here breathes new life into this room.

at left
This Tissue Paper finish will give your wall a leather-like look. Discover how to do this in your own home by reading chapter seven.

This beautiful green kitchen features the Waterfall technique. The look is achieved by applying each of three different color values with a cotton cloth. Look up chapter three for details.

at right
The opulent look of this formal dining room has been achieved through the generous use of silver and gold colors. Chapter eleven gives details so you can do this in your own home.

This Newsprint finish is actually a negative application. In other words, the newsprint is used to remove the white glaze from the blue base coat. Learn to use newsprint in chapter five.

at right
The difference between the sheens in a flat latex paint and a semigloss paint are very apparent in this formal dining room. The colors are exactly the same, only the sheens differ. See how to Wall Stripe in chapter twelve.

This faux Stone Finish conjures up notions of castles and dungeons, but after reading chapter nine
you will be able to recreate this look in your own home—even if it isn't a castle.

at left
There are two effects at work in this formal dining room: Wall Striping and a Tissue Paper finish. To learn how to create a stripe pattern,
read chapter twelve.

BOOKS FOR FURTHER READING

Bennell, Jennifer. *Master Strokes*. Rockport, MA: Rockport Publishers, 1991.

Chijiiwa, Hideake. *Color Harmony: A Guide to Creative Color Combinations*. Rockport, MA: Rockport Publishers, 1987.

Drucker, Mindy, and Pierre Finkelstein. *Recipes for Surfaces: Decorative Paint Finishes Made Simple*. New York: Fireside Publishers (Simon & Schuster), 1990.

Guegan, Yannick, and Roger Le Puil. *The Handbook of Painted Decoration*. New York: W.W. Norton, 1996.

Innes, Jocasta. *The New Paint Magic*. New York: Pantheon Books, 1992.

Marx, Ina Brosseau, Allen Marx, and Robert Marx. *Professional Painted Finishes*. New York: Watson-Guptill Publications, 1991.

SCHOOLS

Prismatic Painting Studio
Gary Lord, David Schmidt, Directors
935 W. Galbraith Rd.
Cincinnati, OH 45231
Phone/Fax: (513) 931-5520
Web address: www.prismaticpainting.com
E-mail: info@prismaticpainting.com

The Finishing School
Bob Marx, Director
50 Carnation Ave., Bldg. 2
Floral Park, NY 11001
Phone: (516) 327-4850
Fax: (516) 327-4853
Web address: www.thefinishingschool.com

Decorative Finishes Studio
Martin Alan Hirsch, Director
1905 Bardstown Rd.
Louisville, KY 40205
Phone: (800) 598-FAUX
Web address: http://www.fauxfinish.com
E-mail: mahirsch@fauxfinish.win.net

The Phoenix Academy
2016 W. North Lane
Phoenix, AZ 85021
Phone: (602) 749-1721,
(888) 323-FAUX
Web address: http:/www.phxacademy.com

Barth's Faux Effects Decorative Finishing Studio
Barth White, Director
3520 W. Coleman St.
Las Vegas, NV 89032
Phone: (702) 631-5959, (800) 998-3289
Fax: (702) 658-9588

Definitive School of Decorative Arts
Reohn Zeleznik, Director
The Resource Center
6010 Washington Ave.
Houston, TX 77007
Phone: (713) 802-9022
Fax: (713) 863-1558
E-mail: info@definitivefaux.com

Ritins Studio Inc.
170 Wicksteed Ave.
Toronto, Ontario M4G 2B6 Canada
Phone: (416) 467-8920
Fax: (416) 467-8963

Faux Effects, Inc.
Raymond P. Sandor, Director
3435 Aviation Blvd. A4
Vero Beach, FL 32960
Phone: (800) 270-8871
Fax: (561) 778-9653

SUPPLIERS

Benjamin Moore & Co.—Paint products available nationwide through dealers.
51 Chestnut Ridge Rd.
Montvale, NJ 07645
Phone: (800) 344-0400

Dover Publications—Write for free crafts and fine arts catalogs.
Dept. 23
31 E. 2nd St.
Mineola, NY 11501

Dressler Stencil Co.—Manufacturer and distributor of pre-cut stencils.
253 SW 41st St.
Renton, WA 98055
Phone: (888) 656-4515
Fax: (425) 656-4381
Web address: http://www.dresslerstencils.com

Faux Effects, Inc.—Manufacturer, distributor and teacher of water-based decorative paint products.
3435 Aviation Blvd. A4
Vero Beach, FL 32960
Phone: (800) 270-8871
Fax: (561) 778-9653

Liberty Paint Catalogue, Inc.—Faux finish brushes, tools, sponges and paint.
P.O. Box 1248
Hudson, NY 12534
Phone: (518) 828-4060

Loew-Cornell, Inc.—Mail order and distributor of artist's and faux brushes.
563 Chestnut Ave.
Teaneck, NJ 07666
Phone: (201) 836-8110

Pratt & Lambert, Inc.—Paints, ready-mix glazes, available nationwide.
P.O. Box 22
Buffalo, NY 14240
Phone: (716) 873-6000

Sepp Leaf Products, Inc.—Mail order gold leaf supplies.
381 Park Ave. S., Suite 1312
New York, NY 10016
Phone: (212) 683-2840

Robert Simmons, Inc.—Artist's brushes.
45 W. 18th St.
New York, NY 10011
Phone: (212) 633-9237

ORGANIZATIONS

Society of Decorative Painters—Membership organization, seminars and instruction books.
P.O. Box 808
Newton, KS 67114
Phone: (316) 283-9665

Stencil Artisans League—Stenciling and faux finish membership organization, seminars and conventions.
10521 Saint Charles Rock Rd.
Suite 1
Saint Ann, MO 63074-1838
Phone: (314) 429-3459
Fax: (314) 429-0334
E-mail: SALISTL@AOL.COM

GLOSSARY

ALKYD: oil-based paint.

AMORPHIC: irregular shape.

BASE COAT: 100 percent paint coverage of a wall surface over which you plan to add a glaze coat or some other painted finish.

BURNISH: to smooth out; for instance, to move excess wallpaper paste from beneath the wallpaper or to rub down tape so it's smooth.

BURNISHING TOOL: a flat stick or other tool (even a credit card) used to safely rub a surface.

CAULK: to fill cracks with filler, usually to correct unsightly gaps where wood trim connects to the wall surface.

CHIP BRUSH: a brush made from white China bristle.

COMBING: a decorative paint finish created by making marks in wet paint with a rubber- or metal-tined comb.

COTTON SHEETING: sheets or similar material made from cotton.

CRACKLE FINISH: a finish that cracks as it dries and gives an aged appearance.

CUT IN: to use a painting brush to apply paint along the edge of the ceiling, door and window frames, baseboards, and corners before you roll on your paint.

DAMASK: a reversible fabric, usually silk or linen, with a figured weave; this creates the subtle value difference in the fabric which creates its pattern.

DISTRESSED TECHNIQUE: makes a surface appear to be older than it is.

FAUX FINISH: literally means "fake" finish; used to describe paint finishes that look like other things; for example, combining paint colors and techniques to make a surface appear to be marble or stone.

GLAZE: a thin film of color applied over a base coat to create a broken color effect. A glaze is made by using part paint, part glazing medium and part appropriate solvent.

GROUT: a fine plaster used between tiles or stone to fill chinks or cracks.

HVLP SPRAYER: high-volume, low-pressure sprayer. Does not atomize the paint so you get less overspray.

JIG: device used to create a repetitive pattern.

LINSEED OIL: oil additive used in paint because of its long drying quality.

METALLIC: consisting or suggestive of metal.

MOTTLED: marked with blotches or spots of different colors or shades.

MUTED: toned down or subtle.

NEGATIVE APPLICATION: taking paint away from a surface, using various tools, each tool creating a different pattern.

OPAQUE: not allowing light to pass through.

PATINA: a mellowed appearance on a surface that suggests age or use.

PETROGLYPHS: primitive, distinctive style of cave painting.

PIGMENT: insoluble coloring matter mixed with oil or water to make paints.

POSITIVE APPLICATION: adding paint to a surface with a variety of tools, each tool creating a different pattern.

RAGGING: using rags to create various decorative paint finishes in either a positive or negative application.

SHEEN: degree of shine on a painted surface when dry.

SOLVENTS: substances used for dissolving another substance.

SPONGING: using a sponge to create various decorative paint finishes in either a positive or negative application.

SQUIRREL MIXER: attachment for a drill that has a plastic cage on the end. It beats and mixes the paint and is especially useful for thick material.

STENCIL: Mylar, tin, plastic or other material cut through in such a way that when paint is applied over it a pattern emerges.

STRIPING: decorative paint finish using a repetitive vertical pattern.

SUBSTRATE WALLPAPER: the wallpaper beneath the finish you are applying.

TRANSLUCENT: allowing light to pass through.

TRANSPARENT: easily seen through.

X-ACTO KNIFE: name brand of a utility knife, available in all hardware stores.

INDEX

A

Alkyd, 126
Amorphic, 126

B

Base coats
    defined, 126
    oil-based paints, 19
    technique, 23
    water-based paints, 18
Blending, 27-30, 31, 48-57, 91
Books, 124
Brushes, 15-16
    chip, 16
    cleaning, 21
    quality, 16
    size, 15
Burnish, 126
Burnishing tool, 126

C

Caulking
    defined, 126
    repairing, 22
Ceilings, protecting, 22
Chalk, 75
Chip brushes, 16
    defined, 126
Choosing a color, 17
Cleanup, 21
Color
    choosing, 17
    combining, 17
    mixing, 17
    theory, 17
Combing, 104-111
    defined, 126
Combining color, 17
Cotton sheeting, 126
Cracked paint, repairing, 22
Crackle finish, 48-57, 115
    defined, 126
Cut in, 126

D

Damask, 126

Dark paneling, lightening up, 36-41,
    117
Definitions, 126
Distressed technique, 126
Drips, 37

E

Education, 124

F

Faux finish, 126
Floors, protecting, 22
Furniture, protecting, 22

G

Gallery, 112-123
Glazes, 110-111
    defined, 126
    newsprint, with, 43
    oil-based paints, 19
    techniques, 23
    tissue paper, with, 62-63
    water-based paints, 18
Glossary, 126
Grout, 126

H

HVLP sprayer, 126

J

Jigs
    defined, 126
    wall striping, 97-99

K

Kraft paper, 67

L

Lightening up dark paneling, 36-41, 117
Linseed oil, 126

M

Metallic textured finish, 90-95, 114
    defined, 126
Mixing color, 17
Mottled, 126
Muted, 126

N

Negative application, 126
Newsprint, 42-47, 120
    glazes, using, 43

O

Oil-based paints, 19
    base coats, 19
    glazes, 19
Opaque, 126

P

Paints, 16
    amount needed, 20
    color. *See* color
    labeling, 21
    oil-based, 19
    sealers, 20
    sheen, 20
    storage, 21
    water-based, 18
Patina, 126
Petroglyphs, 126
Pigment, 126
Positive application, 126
Practicing, 37
Projects, 24-111
    combing, 104-111
    crackle finish, 48-57
    lightening up dark paneling, 36-41
    metallic textured finish, 90-95
    newsprint, 42-47
    sand drift finish, 82-89
    stone block finish, 74-81
    tissue paper finish, 58-65
    torn paper finish, 66-73
    two-color rag blend, 27-30
    wall striping finish, 96-103
    waterfalls, 31-35

R

Ragging, 126
Readings, 124
Room preparation, 22
Rough-sawed wood, staining on, 37
Rubber comb, 1-5
Runs, 37

S

Sand drift finish, 82-89
Schools, 124
Sealers, 20
Sheen, 20, 126
Snap string, 75
Solvents, 126
Sponging, 126
Squirrel mixer, 105
  defined, 126
Staining, 37-39
Stencils, 25, 58-59
  defined, 126
Stone block finish, 74-81, 123
Striping, 126
Substrate wallpaper, 126
Suppliers, 125
Surface preparation, 22
  repairs, 22

T

Techniques
  base coats, 23
  blending, 27-30, 31, 91
  combing, 104-111
  crackle, 48-57, 115
  glaze coats, 23
  lightening up dark paneling, 36-41, 117
  metallic textured finish, 90-95, 114
  newsprint, 42-47, 120
  sand drifts, 82-89, 113
  staining, 37-39
  stencils, 25, 58-59
  stone blocks, 74-81, 123
  tissue paper, 25, 58-65, 116
  torn paper, 66-73, 112, 113
  two-color rag blend, 27-30, 48-57
  wall striping, 96-103, 121
  waterfalls, 31-35, 118

Tissue paper finish, 25, 58-65, 116
Tools
  brushes, 15-16. *See also* Brushes
  cleaning, 21
  paints, 16
Torn paper finish, 66-73, 112
Translucent, 126
Transparent, 126
Trim, protecting, 22
Two-color rag blend, 27-30, 48-57

W

Wall striping, 96-103, 121
Water-based paints, 18
  base coats, 18
  glazes, 18
Waterfalls, 31-35, 118

X

X-acto knife, 126